Franniebell and Purple Wonder

Joann Keder

Franniebell and Purple Wonder

Copyright ©2019 Joann Keder (www.joannkeder.com)

Second Edition ©2022

ISBN 978-1-953270-09-2

Cover Art by Marion Doin

Edited by: Debbie See and Dayle Wallien

Purpleflower Press

First Edition September 2019

Second Edition October 2022

Printed in the United States of America

Also by Joann Keder

Also by Joann Keder:

Piney Falls Mysteries

Welcome to Piney Falls

Saving Piper Moonlight

Tales of Naybor Manor

Lavender's Tangled Tree

The Twisted Stitch Society

Charming Mysteries

Oceanberry Blues

Tangerine Troubles

Perilously Pink

Chaos and Cranberries

Emory Bing Mysteries

(Five bite-sized Mysteries)

Pepperville Stories

The Story of Keilah

Secrets and Sunflowers

The Something That Happened In Pepperville

Be the first to hear about new releases! Sign up for my newsletter here:

http://www.joannkeder.com

Acknowledgments

I am grateful to have an encyclopedia of great people with in-depth knowledge in my life. Rebecca Elliott, Dinah Dahlen, and Jamie Zimlin, thank you for sharing your wisdom with me.

Every single member of my family has contributed to my success in some way. I thank you and I love you.

For my Family
Near and Wide

"I count him braver who overcomes his desires than him who conquers his enemies; for the hardest victory is over self."

Aristotle

Chapter 1

Georgina Hardwick 1974

"DON'T PICK AT your food, Brett. We're not made of cash like some in this town. Money to burn, those people. We eat what we have." Mildred stepped off her stool and brought the pan of steaming noodles to the table.

"I don't want to eat noodles and beans again. Can't we have something else?" six-year-old Brett asked, shoving his plate to the center of the table. On the days she was the most exhausted, she still struggled to tell them apart. But *I* could tell. His twin, identical down to the same seventeen freckles sprinkled across his face, flicked a bean at his brother.

"Calvin, eat your food and quit playing! Bob! Can you help me?" Mildred touched her dark hair, stacked high on her head to give the illusion she was over five feet tall. For a while, she wore platform shoes that Bob brought home from the clearance rack, but soon they caused enough pain that she sacrificed style for comfort.

1

Bob folded the *Pepperville Daily Times* and set it on the table, seemingly oblivious to the chaos. "Where's Georgina? Shouldn't she be eating with us?"

Mildred rolled her eyes. "Up in her room, listening to rock music. Says she's not hungry."

"That's not how things work in our house. We have rules here." Bob got up from the table and straightened his beige tie. He didn't take his tie off until after dinner every night. When I was in fourth grade, I wanted to marry him when I grew up. He was graying at the temples, strong-jawed, and handsome in my weird little mind.

"I'm right here," I said quietly as he strode past me and up the mint green, shag-carpet-covered steps. The beat of my music pulsed, and he took a moment to calm himself before knocking on my door.

"Georgina? It's your father. Open, please." I thought about how long I could play this game. Usually, they tripped over my big feet or discovered my presence in some other unceremonious way.

"Open now, Georgina." I sighed. "Down here, Dad."

My father quickly came down the steps. His thick glasses slid down his nose as he planted himself in front of me. "Why didn't you say something? And why is your music blaring when you aren't even there?"

I let the straps of my tank top slide off my shoulders and fall to the top of my arms—something I knew irritated him. "I came down to get a magazine. I'm writing a report for English on magazine photographers."

He tapped my bare feet, which were draped over the side of the recliner. "Sit up straight. We don't slouch in this house. You're not wearing appropriate clothing for dinner."

I flipped my thick, wavy brown hair to the side. Hair-flipping was also high on his list of unacceptable behavior. "I'm not hungry, Dad. Besides, you always say I look like your mom in the Miss Pepperville 1930 photo. She was wearing less than me."

Bob folded his arms and raised his eyebrows. "She wasn't invited to dinner in that outfit. Now, go upstairs and put something over your undergarments. And turn off that racket. You'll eat with your family."

I rolled my cocoa brown eyes. "Steve Miller Band. It's *not* racket." Some days I didn't have much energy to argue.

He pointed his finger upstairs indicating *"Go!"* and I reluctantly put my homework down. I didn't worry too much about getting my assignments done.

I always had help.

I pulled an extra-long pink t-shirt over my head and purposely stomped down each of the twelve steps to the kitchen, where my brothers were throwing pieces of napkin at each other while my mother propped *The Ladies Weekly Journal* against her plate.

"I told you, I'm not hungry." I plopped down in my seat, throwing the accumulation of napkin bits at Calvin, the most conveniently located twin. We ate the same thing every night. It was a good representation of my life. Monotonous.

"You'll sit with us 'til we're done. That's how we do things here." Bob scooted himself up to his plate and helped himself to a large scoop of noodles. "How was your day, dear?"

3

Mildred closed her magazine and surveyed the table. "We got in a nice box of apples. It was sale day, which means those who don't need it come in and buy like they won't see tomorrow. Do you know that Brownwell woman comes in and spends at least sixty dollars on groceries each time she's at the Shoppe and Walke?"

Bob nodded but didn't bother looking up from his plate.

"My foot is bothering me again. Will you help me pick out better shoes? Everybody thinks having tiny feet is such a blessing. They haven't tried to find comfortable shoes for a long day at work."

"Of course, dear."

"Dad, I've been thinking about getting a camera." I took a sip of the glass of milk beside my plate, hoping the napkin war hadn't reached my drink yet.

I was wrong.

"You have a camera. That pocket-sized thing your grandmother left you. You should be saving your money for college. You know we can't afford extras. If your grandmother would have included us in her will..."

Bob put his hand on Mildred's arm. "Not in front of the children, dear. Why do you need a camera, Georgina?" My mother pulled her arm away but said nothing. Neither of them understood me. Not that they tried.

I sat back in my chair, hands on top of my head. "I can't believe you guys. I've been telling you for a while that I want to be a photographer."

Mildred chuckled. "Daughter, you wanted to be a famous chef just last week."

I could feel my cheeks burning. "I want to do both

of those things. You see all of those pictures of food in magazines? I could make the food *and* take those pictures. Somebody has to do that, y'know."

"Your knowledge of cooking is limited. It's better that you concentrate on your studies for now. Not many people make it to that level. It's better to find a reasonable way to support yourself first. You've had plenty of experience in childcare. What about something in that field?"

The colorful pictures of steaming bowls of soup. Crispy cookies. Even two golden-toasted pieces of bread with bright yellow cheese oozing out from each side. It was a different kind of life than mine. One that had meaning.

I sat silently.

"Your head is in the clouds, Gigi. Most people spend their lives like me: working all day at a cash register. Help me clear the plates now." My mother lowered herself from her regular-sized chair to the floor. As the tallest person in the house, I was needed every night to put the dishes into the cupboards.

The olive green wall phone rang. "Can I answer?

We're technically done eating." Mildred nodded.

"Hardwick residence, Georgina speaking."

I glanced over at my parents and then turned toward the wall, smiling.

Chapter 2

Georgina

"IT'S ME. CAN you sneak out tonight? There's a party four blocks over. Randy Millman's parents are out of town."

Edgar was the best-looking guy in our senior class. He begged me to date him for most of junior year, finally winning me over with his declaration that the two best looking people in the school were fated to end up with each other because that's how it went in all the movies.

I glanced at my parents. Mildred was scraping plates into the trash. Bob was reading the paper. "That *project* may be a timing thing, *Cindy*. Do you know what time it's due?"

"Huh. Cindy's a new one. I like that. Starts at eight."

"Okay, Cindy, I can work on that with you. How about after fourth period?"

"Oh, and wear that top I like. The one without the sleeves."

"Whatever you say, Cindy. I want an A on that

project." I hung up and wasted a fake smile on my parents, who were fully engrossed in their respective activities.

I hurried through the dishes, possibly leaving a stray noodle or two. As soon as I was done, I kissed them goodnight. "I've got a lot of studying to do. Two big tests tomorrow." They always went to bed early on weeknights, so I was allowed to stay up as late as needed to finish my homework.

I ran upstairs and began applying a thick layer of foundation. I didn't mind the orange line between my jaw and neckline; it implied a tan line. Everyone who was considered popular did it. I dug through the pile of clothing on my bed to find the tube top Bob asked Mildred to throw in the trash last week.

The cube-shaped clock on my desk said 7:45. Carefully, I opened the window and placed my foot on the trellis. I'd climbed out so many times, there was a worn spot where my feet went. It was a good thing my father hadn't had time to repaint the peeling white slats of wood, as he had been threatening to do for years.

Every time I reached the ground, I took off on a dead run. If my parents heard any noises, I didn't want to give them the opportunity to discover what was going on before I was off the property. Most girls I knew had been caught at least once.

Not me.

Randy Millman's house was known for parties. His neighbors must've been completely deaf because they never called the police, no matter how many drunken teenagers ended up vomiting on their lawns. I contemplated knocking but instead opened the door and went in.

"Hey, babe! You made it!" Something about Edgar Pepper's dark, brooding face made me melt every time I saw him. His unruly, ebony curls were the same length as some of the girls in my senior class.

I kissed him hard on the lips, the way he liked. His hand slipped to my back and then lower, until he cupped my behind and pulled me in close. I knew other people in the room were staring at us; we were the most attractive couple at Pepperville High. Making out in public was our way of giving them the show they wanted.

"You look great tonight. That's the one I was talking about." Edgar touched my chest. I resisted the urge to pull away.

"Gigi, you want a beer?" My best friend, Lois Masters, was at least a foot shorter than me. If you put a picture of one of us in a thesaurus, the other would be offered as an antonym. Her long, straight blond hair was pulled tightly up in a bun on top of her head. I told her a million times that hairstyle emphasized her "sturdy" build and she'd be better off leaving it down. She reached up to hand me a red, plastic cup.

"Thanks, Lo. Is Jack here?"

Lois pulled her lips back tight, showcasing her strong underbite. "Nope. Probably heard I was here and was afraid to show."

"Oh, stop. He's just shy." I knew better.

"Hey, Gigi, there's an empty room. If you want?" Edgar nuzzled the nape of my neck.

"Would I say no?"

We made our way through the crowd of drunken teenagers, finding one unoccupied room. There were crosses hanging on the wall and a picture of Randy's parents on a church group mission trip to Puerto Rico. His parents possessed that familiar, pinched look of judgment on their faces, just like Bob and Mildred. I smiled broadly, as if they could see me.

Edgar began pulling at my top and I eagerly unbuttoned his pants. "You won't back out this time?" he asked.

"I keep telling you, I just felt weird doing stuff in your bedroom when your parents were home." I rarely told him no.

After removing only the necessary clothing, we ravaged each other for ten minutes. I was always secretly relieved it never lasted longer; my mind always drifted to things other than Edgar. If I'm being honest, sometimes I thought about his friends: what they looked like naked, how they would be tender and loving with me in a way Edgar hadn't mastered.

"We're going to be so great together in San Francisco," Edgar said as he rubbed my arm. "This time next year, we'll be city cats, babe!" He kissed my head in a way that made me feel like he looked at me as his equal, two adults starting life together. "Lots of underground clubs. I'll audition for one of them. That's our in. I've read lots of music producers go incognito, to those unknown places, just to find new talent. You can find a place to take your pictures, too."

"Have you told your parents yet? My parents don't think I'm serious." Technically, I hadn't told them I wasn't going to college. Or that I was planning to live in sin with my boyfriend.

Edgar sat up. "You don't know my dad. He's such a jerk. I'm gonna have to come up with something good. If I could get a job playing in a band, he'd understand how good I am."

I ran my fingers up and down his back, the way he liked. "You *are* good. I love that song you wrote for me, 'Brown Eyes Are My Acid Trip'. I've never heard anyone play guitar like you. I don't think The Steve Miller Band is as good as you."

He moved my hand to a different location on his back. "I wish my dad felt that way. He wants me to stay here and run the implement dealership. He doesn't understand that I'm not like him, or anyone else in the family."

Sometimes I wondered if his dad realized he wasn't as smart as his other sons. I tried to picture Edgar filling out menial paperwork while his brothers did the serious stuff involved in running a business. I sighed. "My dad doesn't listen to reason either—well, both of my parents. They wouldn't believe I could do something like this on my own. They still live in the 1960s."

Edgar pulled me around in front of him and took my head in his hands. "You and me, we're too good for this place. We don't think like everyone else. We've got a bigger vision. Someday people will be looking up Pepperville, Iowa on a map, just to see where we started."

How wrong he was.

Chapter 3

Kenneth Brownwell

"YOU'VE GOT TO stop doing this." Georgina carelessly slammed her locker door, causing those around her to jump.

Mine was two lockers down. I tried to be cool when she was around, but she drove me crazy. The smell of her hair, her big brown eyes, she was like a painting from one of my mother's thick, artsy-type coffee table books. She looked like someone too perfect to be real. I pretended to look at the neat stack of books in my locker, so she wouldn't see me blush.

After chores and dinner, I finished up my homework before doing hers. It all came easy to me and I knew how much she struggled, what with having to take care of her brothers after school and everything. It didn't seem like a big deal.

"I wouldn't have passed calculus last semester without your help. You're dynamite. But you don't have to bail me out every time." She turned to face me, adjusting her low-cut top so that her lacy bra was just visible. I knew she did that to drive boys wild. I didn't care.

"Well, I know you have to babysit every day. I don't have siblings, but from what my mom says, I was quite a handful. And you have two of them." I crossed my arms. There was no way to stand and look cool being as tall and skinny as I was. No one but me wore blue plaid farmer shirts every day. The other kids from farm families knew better than to make it obvious. My mom liked making my shirts and that was her favorite pattern. Whatever my dad and I could do to make her happy, we did.

I touched my wide, white cowboy hat as a group of girls walked by. They rolled their eyes at me. Most of the day, my straight dark hair stayed hidden under the brim of my hat. When I took it off in class, there was an indent around the circumference of my head that caused people to snicker. Seemed better if I left it on. Brownwells look better with a covered head, Dad always said.

Georgina laughed, a loud, unrestrained sound that made me happy every time I heard it. "Oh man, those two. I gave up trying to make them behave. Now I let them run around like two tornadoes until about a half an hour before Mom gets home. Then I clean up and we sit on the couch like nothing's going on 'til she walks through the door. I'm *never* having kids."

I chuckled nervously. "See? That's why I do it. You're a dynamite chick and I'll do whatever I can to make your life easier." I adjusted my gigantic belt buckle; a wide belt was the only thing keeping my pants above waist level.

"Well, thanks. I'll have to learn how to do all of this myself at some point, unless you want to come with me to college." She smiled and touched my arm, knowing full well the electric surges that went through my body every time she did.

"So, where are the big parties this weekend? You and Edgar find some good ones?"

"Yeah. There's one out at Lecher Farm. Kevin's parents are at a cattle auction in Illinois. Lost in Pepperville is going to play and everything. You should go!" She looked away after she said it like she instantly regretted those words. I knew what she thought: *Pathetic Kenneth with no friends.* To be invited to a party where people would make fun of the skinny, rich boy with acne and no social skills was almost cruel.

"Or... I can tell you all about it next week."

"My parents don't normally allow... Yeah, I'll see what I can do." I didn't mind missing parties; I liked my life. I handed Georgina her homework. "You know, even if I can't keep up with your social life, I'll always be there for you, no matter what. Don't forget that, okay?" I looked at her perfect oval face, displaying a sweet, beautiful innocence. I wanted to take it in my hands and kiss her until neither of us could breathe.

"Thanks, Ken," she said uncomfortably. "You're a good guy."

"Hey, babe." Edgar came up from behind and began

13

kissing Georgina on the neck. He tried grabbing her behind, but she caught his hand before he got there.

"Not in the hall! We almost got expelled last time!"

I looked away.

"Hey, Ken. What's shakin'?" Edgar smiled his standard public smile and patted—no, *smacked*—my back. "You still wanna go for a ride in my Superbird? I could take you after school." Just like Edgar, his Signal Red Pontiac Superbird was the most attractive in the school parking lot. It had been a gift from his father for passing junior year.

"I can't... I have chores at the farm, and my folks..."

"Well, maybe next time then. Gigi, I'll walk you to class. I have to talk to you about something." Edgar pulled her in close, her head in the crook of his arm. "Keep on truckin', Ken."

Edgar began guiding Georgina down the hall. "Thanks again, Kenneth!" she called back to me.

I knew things about Edgar. My mom seemed to know everything about everyone and the Pepper family was no exception. "I'll tell you, son, but you can't let your friends know..." I wished I could tell Gigi. She deserved so much more.

We had freshman P.E. together. Everyone made fun of my skinny white legs. While I was working the fields of Brownwell Farm with my dad all summer, they were splashing at the pool and giggling with their friends without a care in the world. Mom went in and tried to get them to change their shorts-only policy, but the principal said it was necessary, no matter how much

Mom mentioned she knew things about his daughter and her drinking and driving.

The only person to choose me for a dodgeball team was Gigi. "Stand by me, Kenneth. We'll put those suckers on their knees." From that day on, she watched out for me. Never let any of the popular kids say a bad word, and if they did, she'd make them sorry. Until Edgar came around, that is.

He chased after her for six months, possibly longer, kept telling her she was the only one up to his standards. I knew all about his standards. Mom told me. Gigi finally gave in. Maybe he has a magic power I don't know about. She hasn't been the same since.

Chapter 4

Georgina

I PULLED AWAY from Edgar's grip around my neck and grabbed his hand. "What's going on?"

"My dad said I have to work at the dealership tomorrow."

Edgar's father owned the largest farm implement dealership in the state. Pepper's Implement-Ville— *you plow, we wow.* His father was a relentless businessman, even working in his own home to sell his way of life.

"I thought your brother traded you for next weekend so he could go to some event with Julia?"

Edgar rolled his eyes. "They're not talking to each other. Happens every other week or so. They always put on a good show for my folks and then go home and throw appliances at each other. So now I'm stuck until at least four, unless I can pretend I'm sick and go home early. My mom digs that. She thinks they work me too hard. Kevin Lecher's cousin's band is playing at that party and they are short a guitarist. Kevin heard I play, so he asked me to fill in."

I stopped. "What? You got asked to play for Lost in Pepperville? Really? That's rad! I can't believe it, babe." I rubbed his back, a tiny bit jealous that things were working out for him. "Wow."

"I told you. We're on our way. You and me in San Francisco. They'll be talking about us for years to come."

I smiled. "I can't wait. My parents don't believe I can do anything but take care of stupid brats. They'll be so embarrassed. When I come home to visit, I might not even stop at their place. I'll stay at the Pepperville De Splendour and order room service every day."

"I'm not coming back." Edgar smiled broadly. "Once I'm gone, they can read about me in the papers. Wrinkled old Dander will fill her drawers thinking about the guy she called 'a waste of a beating heart' making it big."

As we reached my classroom, Edgar pulled me in close. Advanced English IV teacher, Agnes Dander, stood inside the doorway, unrepentant in her glee about blocking the doorway to prevent his entrance. "Mr. Pepper, you've got somewhere else to be, I presume? Your remedial class met earlier in the day."

Edgar put his thumb to his ear and his pinky finger to his lips and mouthed the words, "Call me."

I nodded and blew him a kiss before sliding in next to Lois at the table. "Can I say I'm spending the night at your house again?" I whispered.

"You never actually showed up last time. I thought you'd come in through the window at some point. I was up all night waiting." Lois looked at me skeptically. "I mean, I'm the one who has to lie to your parents when they call looking for you."

I blushed, looking down at my books sheepishly. Edgar and I fell asleep in his car after several steamy rounds and I didn't want to knock on Lois's window so late. I figured I was being polite. "Sorry."

Ever since I started dating Edgar, we followed the same routine. Lois's mother knew how strict Bob and Mildred were and she took pity on me. She reluctantly agreed to lie for her daughter's friend if she was forced but made it clear she preferred for the arrangement to be between me and Lois.

Being popular had its perks. I realized how important I was to Lois in her mother's eyes; her daughter was pretty and popular when she was with me, just by proximity. Lois's mom was convinced her daughter would spend her life alone if she didn't find a serious boyfriend in high school.

"I can't leave home until at least eight, and Lost in Pepperville won't start playing 'til nine. I promise we can go home together whenever you have curfew. I'll just see you out there?"

"Pinkies?" Lois offered her little finger.

"Pinkies."

My usual routine was to stop by Pepperville Elementary on my way home. I arrived in time to see Calvin and Brett wrapping the chain from a swing around the neck of a classmate.

"Boys! Leave that poor little girl alone!" I ran as quickly as I could to the swings, pushing the boys out of the way. I unwrapped the sobbing girl and sat down on the gravel beside her. "You okay, little goddess?" I pulled her in close, stroking her tangled blonde hair. "Boys, you treat this girl like a princess from now on or I will set fire to your toys, one by one. Dig it?"

Calvin kicked a little bit of gravel at me, and I reached over and grabbed his leg. "Do you remember the last time you did that? What did I do?"

"You sat on me until I cried."

"That's right. Tell this girl you're sorry. Both of you."

"Sorry," they both muttered.

"Now start walking home. I'll meet you there."

The boys walked slowly until they reached the cement sidewalk. "Race me!" Brett challenged. Both took off in a dead run.

It was the one point in the day I allowed myself to daydream. San Francisco types all had their lives perfectly planned out, serious yet fun. They all wore current style trends and ate foods I had never heard of. This would be my new everyday life. I would learn how to cook things with foreign spices and exotic names like "marsala" and "carbonara". Steaming, beautiful plates of goodness and new experiences. And then, when I was done cooking, I would photograph my work in the most stylish way possible. Maybe I would move on to fashion models at some point, though I didn't know what kind of camera that would take. Edgar always wanted to model for me, but his idea of pictures didn't seem like anything I could sell to *The Ladies Weekly Journal. Stimulating conversation over complex foods. Walking on the beach. No boring parents or unruly twins. Just me and Edgar, staring lovingly in each other's eyes...*

The boys had an internal alarm. All three of us Hardwick children did. At 4:45 p.m. we began to pick up, clean up, and change our demeanor. When Mildred

Joann Keder

arrived home from a long day at the Shoppe and Walke, we were all sitting on the couch, watching *Batty Bunny* reruns.

Mildred came in the back door and slipped off her shoes, making a grunting sound. "I got some cheese for tonight's noodles. Georgina, will you get the big pot down for me, please?"

Once I move to San Francisco, I'm never eating a noodle again.

"You know we have that early dinner at Pete's Diner with Miss Castle tomorrow. Hopefully, we can smooth over the 'paste in her hair' incident," Mildred said as I spooned canned corn onto her plate. "You can wait on the boys' baths until I get home if you want."

"What time will you be back?"

She looked at Bob, who for once was invested in what was going on. "I don't foresee us being out past eight." He folded the paper and put his hand through his salt-and-pepper grey hair.

I let out a sigh. Bob looked at me with surprise. "Did you have some plans for the evening, Cinderella? We can make it 7:45 if necessary." He chuckled. "I'm sure I can find you a glass slipper from the store."

"Lois asked if I could spend the night."

"At eight o'clock? That's rather late, dear." Mildred folded her arms. "Don't you think, Bob?" She mentioned several times that she didn't approve of Lois's single mother and considered her parenting methods too lenient. That was a big part of the reason she allowed Lois to visit so often—she thought she was doing her a favor.

"Well, we are technically keeping her home until then. And it is the weekend. I suppose you can go."

I tried not to smile. Any time I allowed my parents to see that I truly enjoyed something, it was another tool they could use to control me. "I'll be home by ten the next morning. I'll get all of the laundry done and clean up my room. I promise. Can

I call Lois and let her know?" Bob nodded.

Forgetting my attempt to play things cool, I leapt up from the table and grabbed the phone off the wall, impatient with the slow whirl of the dial.

"Lois? I can come. I'll be there at eight-thirty."

"That's perfect. We might start playing by then if the drummer finishes his court-ordered trash collection by the highway early," Edgar replied on the other end.

"Tell her it may be a bit later. Depending on how poorly the conversation goes," Bob called. "Boys! Noodles are not to be squished through your fingers!"

The following night, we—the boys and I—were settling into Channel 89's presentation of *The Fuzzy Felines of Chatworth* when my parents walked in.

"It's only seven. What are you doing home so early?"

Mildred stepped out of her shoes and climbed onto the couch. "Miss Castle had to bring her nephew with her to dinner. He's apparently got an issue with pickles. She let him order the cheeseburger with extra pickles and it wasn't ten minutes before he was urping all over the place." She sighed. "I don't know if we made any progress or not. I guess we'll see when the boys get their next report card."

I already had my shoes on and had one arm in the sleeve of my coat. "Can I go?"

"Yes. Home by ten. Remember your manners.

Tell your father goodbye on your way out." I bent down and kissed her. "Thanks, Mom."

She looked up, surprised. "Well, yes. Of course."

I walked out the garage door, where my father had the hood of the green station wagon raised. "Heading out?" he asked. "There were some rumblings I didn't like on the way home. This isn't a good month for the car to be in the shop. Thought I'd see what I could do here."

"You could ask Edgar Pepper's dad," I offered.

"He fixes all sorts of equipment at the dealership."

"Yes, I suppose I could," Bob replied halfheartedly.

"Bye, Dad."

I was careful to head towards Lois' house for half a block before doubling back and cutting through the alley on Drake Street. If I stood on Main Street long enough, someone would be willing to drive me the three miles out in the country to the farm. It wasn't more than ten minutes before last year's valedictorian pulled over in his sputtering butter yellow pickup.

"Lecher?" he asked. I nodded.

"Hop in."

When I arrived, it appeared that most of the high school was already there. "Has anyone seen Edgar?" I yelled over the loud drinking games.

"He's in Kevin's bedroom warming up," David, whom I had briefly dated during the summer months, offered. "Do you want a beer?"

"No thanks. I have to be home early tonight." I owed Lois's mother my sobriety at least. I pushed my way through the throngs of high schoolers, past the keg, and up the stairs. When I first started attending parties, I felt uncomfortable just entering homes of people I didn't know. Now that I had been going with Edgar for most of a year, it seemed almost natural to walk into someone's bedroom to make out or smoke weed.

I wasn't really in the mood to listen to his warmups, but he liked that I clapped after each one. I found the door covered in space movie posters and opened it up. It was unusual for him to warm up in the dark, but he was always trying new methods to improve his sound. The dark brown bedspread was on the floor. "Babe?" I asked softly. Maybe I was in the wrong place. There were strange sounds and I allowed my eyes a moment to adjust to the dim light. What I saw shocked me more than anything had in my previous seventeen years and eight weeks of living.

Edgar's arm laid on top of the sheet, resting on the bare leg of my best friend, Lois.

I gasped. "What the *hell*?"

"Gigi, I can explain!" Lois sat upright, unaware of all that she was exposing. "Jack showed up with Dorilynne. Edgar saw how upset I was and he invited me to listen to him practice. I'm so sorry, it just happened!" When my gaze fell to her sorry excuse for a chest, Lois realized she was naked and abruptly pulled the sheet up to her chin.

I looked around the room, seeing the familiar pile of hastily discarded clothing on a chair too far for them to reach. I took their belongings and threw them into the hallway, where curious partygoers had gathered. Edgar's car keys to his Superbird fell out of his pocket as his pants went flying. "I'll be taking these," I said as I slammed the door shut. I wasn't sure what I would do with the car, but it was his prized possession and I needed him to hurt as much as I did.

I ran down the stairs, eyes stinging with makeup-filled tears and found David, who offered me his foamy drink. "I don't want a beer. Do you have anything stronger?"

David went to the kitchen and returned with a plastic cup, filled with a red liquid. "I don't know what's in here, but it's pretty safe to say there's nothing left in his parents' liquor cabinet. Everything cool, Gigi?"

I grabbed the cup from his hand and gulped down the entire sweet, syrupy-slushy mess in one gulp. "Get me more," I demanded. David handed me the one he had in his hand and I walked outside, behind the barn, where Edgar's freshly-waxed red car sat at a distance from the other vehicles.

I resisted the immediate urge to beat it with a loose board. Instead, I plopped into the driver's seat, with the window rolled down, drinking slowly this time, trying to absorb the situation. *My boyfriend and my best friend? Was he just playing me all along? Anything to get me to sleep with him? What about San Francisco? Is he taking Lois instead?*

The yard lights flickered on and off, making me slightly dizzy, Maybe I would throw up all over Edgar's car. That would be perfect. I stuck my fingers down my throat.

"Gigi? Is that you?"

I pulled my fingers out and tried to focus on the tall figure standing outside the car door. "Kenneth? Brownwell? What are you doing at a party?" He was dressed in a button-up, collared grey shirt and he had combed his hair. He might have passed for any other high school student. "And what's that smell? You're wearing cologne?"

Kenneth put his hands in his pockets. "You said I should come. So, I went out and bought a new shirt and put on some Manly, just like my dad wears on special occasions."

"Well, you smell dandy." I leaned my head back. "Just dandy."

"Is everything okay, Georgina? You don't seem like you're okay. Can I do something for you?"

I tried to focus on Kenneth, but he was fuzzy. The only part of my brain that was functioning clearly was the part that was set on revenge. "Get in," I commanded.

Kenneth dutifully went over to the passenger side and opened the door.

"No, the backseat," I barked. Slowly, I raised myself from the seat and got out. My head was spinning. I was glad I only had to take a couple of steps before I landed in the back seat beside him.

"Now take off your pants."

"What?"

"You asked what you could do for me. There's only one thing that will make this pain go away. I want you to have sex with me. That's what you can do."

Kenneth clasped his hands together. "That doesn't seem right. You don't seem normal. I don't want to take advantage..."

"Do you want to help me or not? 'Cause if you don't,

I'll find some other dude who will. Then you can sit back and feel bad because you didn't do anything at all to make me better. Is that what you want?"

Kenneth obediently began fiddling with that big belt buckle, which I could now see clearly said BROWNWELL FARM across the middle. I became impatient and pushed his hands out of the way, pulling his belt so violently it almost ripped the loops off his pants. I took my clothes off and guided him the way Edgar had taught me. It was only two minutes, maybe less, but I didn't want to stop because that meant I had to think about them again. My best friend and my boyfriend together. I kissed Kenneth hard, the way Edgar kissed me. His lips were soft and warm. I felt a sweetness emanating from him.

"I'm sorry. I've never done this before. I wasn't prepared..."

"Shhh...." I laid my head on his chest. "No talking."

The car windows began to rattle as Lost in Pepperville played "Baby Stole My El Camino", the one song of theirs Edgar could play without looking at the notes. His high voice could be heard in the chorus. "Shift, shift, shift it low..."

"That's him. Stupid him," I muttered. Tears flowed down my face.

Kenneth gently stroked my hair. "It's okay. I'm here for you, Gigi..."

I sat up abruptly, hitting his nose with my head.

"I'm gonna be sick."

Chapter 5

Georgina

THE ANSWERING MACHINE beeped loudly.

"Georgina? It's Lois again. I just wanted to... to tell you how sorry I am for the... the incident. Can you call me back?"

"Don't you want to talk to her? It sounds important." Mildred shoved the laundry basket full of clean clothes into my room with her foot. "Should I contact her mother? I'm happy to have a discussion about proper behavior if I need to."

I rolled over onto my side and stared at my closed curtain. "I'm not going to talk to her again, Mom. We're not friends anymore."

Mildred walked over to the window, reaching on her tiptoes, and opened the curtains. "Maybe you should give her a chance to explain whatever it is. Good friendships are hard to find. Even harder to keep as long as yours."

I rolled my eyes. "This isn't 1960. Things don't work

like that anymore. Most people have three best friends in a school year." I laid back on my elbows. "It's time for me to grow up. Now that I'm going to college for real... I mean going to college... I'll be making other friends."

Mildred studied my face for a minute. "Well, in any event, we don't just toss good people aside. When I was growing up, everyone made fun of me. Sometimes they tried stacking books on my head to see if they would stay. They called me all sorts of horrible names and there were times when I didn't even feel safe walking down Main Street. If it weren't for my best friend, Shirleen, I wouldn't have survived."

"I know, Mother. You've told me that story a hundred times. Where is your best friend now? It seems like if you had been such good friends, she'd still be in your life today."

Mildred placed her hands on her hips. "That's an entirely different story."

"You always say that, Mom, but you never tell me what happened."

"Put your clean clothes away and then come downstairs and help me dust above the cabinets."

When we returned to school on Monday, Lois was waiting at my locker. "I don't want to talk to you ever again. Shouldn't you be hanging out with your new man?" I shoved Lois aside and did my combination as quickly as I could. I took my books and slammed the door shut, realizing too late that I had removed the wrong ones. I turned abruptly and walked away. Someone would let me look off their books today.

The horror of that night filled my head once again. I spent the night in Shelly Letcher's bedroom, staring at the pink clouds painted on the walls when I wasn't running to the bathroom to throw up. Kevin took me home early the next morning. For the first time, I was climbing up the trellis to my bedroom window.

"Wait! Gigi! Let me tell you what happened!"

I stopped briefly, flipping my middle finger at her, and then turned around to continue walking down the hall. My body hit something solid, which I realized was Kenneth Brownwell. When I looked up, I saw the bump on his nose where I'd accidentally hit him during our fast and furious romp on Saturday.

"Oh, sorry man. I didn't see you there." I hadn't thought about Kenneth since that night. He'd served a purpose. That was all.

"I enjoyed a... special time with you. Thanks for... everything." He put his hands in his pockets, rocking nervously back and forth.

I was mortified. Most likely he would tell everyone, if he hadn't already. "Kenneth, let's just keep this between us. Sometimes things happen at parties that we don't want to make public. Is that cool?" Kenneth looked around the hall. "Did you tell someone? I always thought a lady didn't want to talk about that kind of stuff. I wrote something for you though..."

"No! Kenneth—Ken." He was infuriating. "I don't want you talking about what happened in Edgar's car. To anyone. Got it?"

Kenneth nodded. He shoved the crumpled-up piece of paper deep into his back pocket. "I'll see you after class then! At the lockers!"

"Sure." I would have to figure out how to deal with Kenneth. He would do anything for me though, so I shouldn't have to work too hard. Maybe now was the time to feel bad about using him that night, but I didn't.

I made it through most of the day without seeing Edgar. I didn't return to my locker. One of the perks of being the best-looking girl in school was that every guy would do anything I asked and every girl wanted to be seen with me, even if that meant going without their books during class so I could use them.

As I began walking home, I heard the loud sound of Edgar's muffler pulling up behind me. He honked his ridiculously loud horn. "Hey, I would recognize that ass anywhere. Best looking in town."

I turned around and glared. *He's not worth it*, I thought. I kept walking.

He continued driving beside me, honking insistently. "Hey! I'm talkin' to you. Dammit, Gigi. Stop for a minute."

I threw my books—actually, Tom Watkins' books— at his door. "What do you want from me?"

"Hey! Watch the paint!" Edgar reached over and unlatched the door. "Get in!"

I reluctantly opened the door and sat inside, keeping one foot on the sidewalk. "You have thirty seconds."

"I looked all over for my keys! I had crazy ideas that you drove it into Ashton Lake or something. Didn't get home until 2:00 am. Man, my dad was hacked off. Threatened to take away the car for a month."

I looked at the backseat, where I'd taken Kenneth's virginity without a thought and then tossed the Superbird keys in the chicken coop. Now Edgar's coat and a packet of sample senior pictures sat innocently on that very spot.

"Is that all you can think about? Your damn keys? You were in bed with my best friend." Tears raced down my face. "I believed in you!"

"I was feelin' bad. Jack told her he didn't want anything to do with her anymore. I asked if we could talk, and one thing led to another. It wasn't on purpose. You know you're all I want, Gigi."

I couldn't control my tears and they became a full-fledged flood. "Lois is—*was*—my best friend!

Doesn't that mean anything? How many others have there been? Like, someone different every time I can't sneak out?"

"Lois was the only one. I was nervous about my set and I had to release all that energy. You know I can't mess up our plans to go to San Francisco. It won't happen again. You're my babe." He took his fingers and gently massaged the back of my neck before he began kissing me. "Get in and I'll show you how sorry I am."

There was no denying what I felt for him. In the past, I broke up with boyfriends when I tired of them, but with Edgar it was different. We were always in sync, never needing to spend time talking. He made me feel beautiful, that together we were perfect and capable of anything.

Edgar drove to one of our favorite make-out spots on Honeyspill Road. There were several houses that were framed up when Pepperville had its growth spurt in 1968. A rendering plant promised to bring large numbers of people into town, so an enterprising builder began to erect homes. When the city council decided they didn't want that many outsiders overtaking their city at once, the buildings and hopes for a more diverse Pepperville were abandoned. Now it was just three paved streets filled with teenagers in various stages of undress.

After fifteen minutes in the back seat, I felt better about my fling with Kenneth. The experiences canceled each other out, I was sure of it. Poor, sweet Kenneth. Someday he would find just the right girl, someone of equal popularity. They would be happy in their matching blue farm shirts.

"I'm better than Lois, right?"

"No comparison." Edgar pulled me in closer and nibbled on my ear. "Again?"

Chapter 6

Lois

GIGI WAS MY best friend since fifth grade. We were the two smartest girls in the class, always finishing our work together. We were also the tallest and shortest girls in the class—Yin and Yang, our teacher said. It seemed that from the first time I went over to Gigi's house, her mother appreciated my Yang.

"Do you have a hard time reaching things too?" Mildred asked excitedly. "It's definitely not a world for the short-statured."

"My mom and I are both short, but we don't have tall helpers like you do." I smiled. Though my mom and I were five feet and Mildred stood at four-foot, six inches, I understood. I also understood Mildred's type.

I worked weekends at Flowers, Flowers, and Fudge with my mom. She made the floral arrangements and I worked the counter, cutting thick slices of fudge for everyone who came in. There were several customers who were "crusty". By that, I mean closed off on the surface but nice underneath. No matter how nastily the conversation began, I always ended up with a tip. "Lois," my mom always said, "you can turn the sour milk fresh again." I had a gift.

Mildred had a reputation around town as being "sour milk". She didn't like small talk and rarely smiled at customers at the Shoppe and Walke. I took it as a personal challenge to get her on my side. Things were going great until she learned that my mom was a single mother.

After several prodding questions, I admitted that I didn't know for sure who my father was. My mom said those questions were better left unanswered, especially because Pepperville was a small town where everyone knew everyone and it might cause uncomfortable situations for her daughter.

"You'll have to find yourself a decent man and make a good family for yourself," Mildred commented more than once. I knew what she meant. Try to erase my status as a bastard. It didn't bother me though. Most of those comments just rolled off my back like beads of water.

Thanks to my short stature and easy-going nature, I was one of the few welcome guests in the Hardwick home. Gigi invited me over every weekend. Sometimes I helped her with chores, or we would just sit in her room and listen to records.

When we got into junior high, Gigi developed breasts, an amazing body, and an outgoing personality. I had none of those things. She was invited everywhere—to every popular girl event and anything where the boys could stare at her. Most of the time, she tried to make sure I was invited too. Sometimes she just made up excuses about why we couldn't get together, each of us understanding the truth on some level, that even with Gigi by my side I would be uncomfortable.

I didn't even try finding friends of my own. I relished being in the company of the most popular girl in school.

Just like my mother, my aunt, and every Masters woman before her, I developed a large waist. I tried covering it up with long, fringed vests, but I could still feel that embarrassing roll around my middle. I tried starving myself for a while, but I never looked quite the way I wanted: like I matched her. No matter what I did, I could feel Gigi slipping away from me and I didn't like it.

When Gigi started dating the long-haired, loud-mouthed Edgar Pepper, I faked enthusiasm. "Isn't he a stud?" Gigi would say on the rare occasions we walked home together, me taking two steps to every one of Gigi's.

"So cool. He reminds me of Kurt Russell. If he had dark hair and a darker complexion. And probably louder." I half-smiled. I flipped my stringy, long hair behind my shoulder. One of the million things I envied was her wavy-thick hair. Nothing like my thin, lifeless, blonde clump.

"We're going out this weekend. Should I ask someone for you, and we can double date?"

Most girls would turn down a pity date, but I craved

the attention. I would take it wherever I could find it. Maybe I was lazy. I knew I didn't have what came naturally to other girls, so this was the easiest way to get attention. Georgina could make any male bend to her will and it made me feel a little powerful, if only secondhand.

"Sure. Just not that Jefferson kid again. He smelled so bad."

Georgina guffawed. "Oh right. I forgot. Like my brothers' hamper. I'll find someone good for you. Edgar's dad just bought him a car. We can cruise around. Edgar's brother will buy us beer too. Maybe wine. There's a new kind in the box that's like strawberry Kool-Aid."

"Is Edgar old enough to drive? I thought he was like us, not sixteen 'til next year." I didn't like getting into the car with Edgar behind the wheel. He was unpredictable. Especially after he had been drinking.

"Oh, his dad doesn't care. He's been driving since eighth grade, taking parts out to farms for his dad." On Saturday at 7:00 p.m., I knocked on Gigi's door. Mildred answered, dressed in footed pajamas and carrying a cup of cocoa.

"Oh, sweetie, come on in. The boys went fishing with their father, so I'm having myself a cozy night in. Do you want to sit on the couch and wait for Georgina?" I didn't like lying to Mildred. Our relationship was a friendship of some sort. She had been mostly kind and didn't deserve dishonesty.

"No, thanks. I'll sit outside and wait. It's nice and the mosquitos haven't come out yet." I sat down on the concrete porch, pulling my skirt tightly around my ankles.

"Hey! You could've come up!" Gigi opened the door, looking resplendent in her bell-bottom jeans, pink button-down shirt tied just above her waist, and brown wedge sandals. She was wearing dark blue eye shadow and her hair was curled so that it lapped in and out around her face. Just like a model. "Bye, Mom. I'll be home by eleven."

"Tell Dori's mother hello for me," Mildred called from the couch.

"Uh-huh." Georgina pulled the door shut.

"I told her Dori was having some people over. Haven't used her for a while, so it sounded plausible." She pulled her coat over her shoulders and unbuttoned the top two buttons of her shirt.

"They're going to wait for us around the corner."

Yin and Yang, we walked out of sight of 1415 Chesapeake Street and around the corner to Ashton Avenue where Edgar's Superbird was parked, engine revving. There were two heads in the front seat. My heart skipped a beat.

When we walked up, the door swung open. It was Mike, the semi-smart guy who actually read the assignments in history class.

He flashed me a smile and pulled the latch for the back seat. "Ladies first. We've got the best seats back here."

I nodded. Georgina hopped in the front and scooted over, practically on Edgar's lap. She shoved her hand between his thighs.

Joann Keder

"You wanna beer?" Mike asked, pulling one from under the seat.

"Sure." I hated beer.

Edgar drove to Honeyspill Road, where he turned the engine off and the music up. His car had an eight-track player, the most expensive on the market. His father told him it was an advance present for graduation.

I stupidly allowed my gaze to reach the front seat, where Edgar was pushing Gigi's shirt off her arms. I gulped.

"So, Mike, do you like history?" It felt stupid and smart at the same time. "Do you like a certain time period?"

"Umm, yeah, I guess. I like Roman history." Mike looked out the window.

"Oh, I like Imperial Rome..."

"Do you wanna make out? Gigi said you were into that."

"Umm, okay." I awkwardly put my hands around Mike's neck. He shoved his tongue into my mouth and began feeling under my dress. *This is fine. This is great*, I told myself. *It's completely normal for girls my age.* When he got to my waist, I impulsively grabbed his hand and pushed it away. We slid apart and drank our beers silently, waiting for the X-rated theater in the front to cease. It was just like every other double date. A complete bomb.

I wished I could be like Gigi. Unashamed of her body. Able to be passionate with anyone, no matter where. Mike must've been hoping I would be just like Georgina under her dress. I didn't want to give him the

38

satisfaction of knowing there wasn't anyone like Georgina. After that night, I turned down offers for blind dates. I wasn't popular but I was smart.

The day of the Lecher Farms party started out on the wrong foot. I had a moment of strength or weakness, I was never sure which, and decided to wear a tube top. Other girls were doing it, so I felt like I was entitled to wear one as well. As I was walking out of biology, happy that I was the only one in class who aced the test, a sophomore ran up to me and yanked my top down. Probably on a dare. Embarrass the short fat girl because she hasn't had enough. Everyone laughed, and even though I knew it didn't matter, it did, especially when I realized Jack was watching with curiosity. He was still the man of my dreams, even though he hadn't shown any interest in months. It was mortifying.

For the rest of the day, I wore my PE shirt, as smelly as it was, over my tube top. No one said anything but I knew that they were laughing behind my back. As I walked home, I thought about what a relief it was to be alone.

If it were last year, Georgina would have put her arm around my shoulder protectively as we walked home. I would have told her that it didn't matter what those fools did. Friendship was more important than high school boys.

I would never be Georgina. I was Lois, the unpopular girl whose mother couldn't afford braces for her crooked teeth or dance lessons so I could try out for cheerleader. Smart, funny, and yes, even pretty when the light caught her just right. No one seemed to notice.

The one friend I thought would be around forever

was lost to creepy Edgar. Kenneth told me he knew Edgar was sleeping with other girls. I believed him. Kenneth was pure and honest, not like the other boys in our class who were immature and stupid. It wouldn't do any good to tell Gigi—she was lost to his sweet talk and promises of a life together.

I kicked the tire of Mr. Saum's car, which was parked next to my driveway. It was my usual release. He was an awful neighbor. When I was twelve and went to collect money for my paper route, he always winked as he handed me the payment. "One extra dollar for your hard work. Now don't go spend that on candy. Your clothes barely fit the way things are." I never felt bad about kicking his car or dropping peanut shells on his lawn.

Someone honked, jolting me. "Hey, Lois. You goin' to the party tonight?" I had been so immersed in my anger I hadn't heard his car from the standard two-block noise radius. I walked up to his window, feeling awkward without Gigi there to translate to dumb hunk for me.

"Where's Gigi?"

"Just dropped her off. She's gonna be late for the party tonight. I'm playing with Lost in Pepperville. You gonna be there?"

It felt strange that Edgar would care whether I went anywhere. "Ok, yeah. Maybe. Lecher Farm?" I realized it was ridiculous to think I could go anywhere. I had no car.

"Well, I could give you a ride. That cool with you?"

I have moments where my common sense seems

to leave my body. It's not an out-of-body experience. It's more like a loss-of-consciousness with my eyes open. It was wrong to be alone with Edgar. But it felt so flattering to be asked.

"Yeah, fine. What time?"

"Six-thirty, so I can warm up. Far out. I'll pick you up here."

Edgar sped off before I could reply. I thought for a minute about calling Gigi, just to make sure she knew. It hit me that the reason he asked me to go with him was because he hated walking into parties by himself. That was one of the first things Gigi had confided weeks into their relationship. "Edgar would rather bring a total stranger than go into a room by himself. Isn't that mysterious?" *No, it's just weird.*

I looked through my closet, thinking about the clothes Georgina told me accentuated my best features and hid the rest. I pulled out a bright red dress and a thick, black belt. My brown suede boots—the ones Gigi's dad gave me from the extra-super clearance rack —still fit, just barely. I put on all the accumulated makeup in my drawer and stood back, staring at the mirror with satisfaction.

"Oh, baby," Mom gasped. "My goodness, you look almost regal!"

"Thanks, Mom."

"Do you have a date? You didn't mention anyone. Is Georgina setting you up again?" I felt a twinge of resentment that she didn't trust me to find a date on my own.

"Yes. I'm going out with Jack."

"Oh? I thought that was done."

I pined for Jack for months. After we had gone out twice, he flirted with me at every party and then went on to flirt with other girls. He was perfect in

every way my mom would want him to be— handsome, smart, and seriously thinking about becoming a doctor. Gigi tried to set me up several times but Jack would never commit.

I was forced to make up stories so my mom wouldn't think I was pathetic. "Jack needs a little break. We're going to see other people."

"You smell good," I blurted as I hopped into the passenger seat next to Edgar. I immediately wished I could take it back. That wasn't something you said to someone else's boyfriend.

"Oh, thanks. It's *Manly*. My brother lets me borrow it."

He was good looking. I hated to admit that. His hair was just past his broad shoulders and his face looked like that of a movie star. He even had bushy sideburns like the stars in all the magazines. Unlike most of the boys in the senior class, he possessed a hint of a mustache. He looked at least twenty.

"Did you talk to Gigi? Is she still able to watch me?"

My heart sank. "She's coming later. Her parents have something going on, so she has to babysit first."

"Yeah, she's always stuck. No kids for me, man. I'm gonna live a free life, without chains."

We rode in silence the rest of the way, Edgar parking the car between two big, red barns. He pulled up far enough so that other cars wouldn't be able to park beside him.

"Did you know barns are painted red to kill fungus and moss?" I asked. "Just a little bit of trivia."

"Huh. Weird." Edgar shut his door. "You're like some freaky encyclopedia chick."

We walked in together, just like he wanted. Immediately, I moved to the far side of the room, gulping down the first alcoholic drink I could find. It was awful, but I didn't care.

Jack walked in with Dorilynne, holding her tightly at the waist. Another paper doll with perfect makeup and no personality. I was twice as smart as Dori. I was funnier too.

"Hey, Jack!" I said with fake enthusiasm. I hoped he had forgotten what happened earlier in the day; then I decided to sacrifice dignity for a laugh. "You saw enough of me today we should consider it our second date!"

Jack let out a little chuckle. "You're okay, Lois. I wouldn't have taken it that well." He tapped my beer with his own.

I blushed. "Thanks."

"I was crushed at first, but..."

"You need to leave," Dorilynne growled. "Go find yourself a matching troll boyfriend. This one's mine."

I looked at Jack who shrugged his shoulders and took a big gulp of his beer.

"Lots of hot trolls at these types of parties," I said, trying desperately to make a dignified exit. I felt like nothing. A nobody. I thought about all the time I spent getting ready and how pointless it had been. I found a freshman, someone who would be willing to spend time with a senior of any status. I was telling him about the horrors of sophomore year P.E. classes when I felt a tap on the back.

"Hey, Lois, could you help me with something?" It was Edgar.

"Ok, sure." I followed him up the stairs and into an orange bedroom with family pictures on the dresser. It was a relief to have a break from the scrutiny of Dorilynne and every person who had seen what happened to me in the hall.

"Can you rub my shoulders? Gigi always rubs them before I play. It makes me looser and I can play better."

I was shocked and slightly repulsed. It seemed very wrong, but I didn't know how to say so. "Ok, I guess." I set my beer beside the bed and began to rub his shoulders the way my mother taught me.

"Oh, that's it. Right there. Perfect. Just a little harder."

After a long day of working at Flowers, Flowers, and Fudge, Mom needed a release. Massage was another something I was good at because she asked almost every night for a shoulder rub.

"Ok, a little more in that spot."

I tried to distract myself by looking at the pictures on the dresser. The whole family, apart from the oldest son, Kevin, displayed sour expressions on their faces. They didn't seem like the type of people who would appreciate people having a party in their home. They would be horrified to discover these strangers traipsed through their bedrooms, eating their food, and sat on their toilets. I wondered how well Kevin Lecher would clean the place before they came home. He would leave something behind. One beer bottle, at least. Suddenly I realized that Edgar had begun rubbing my arm as I massaged him. I knew I should stop.

"You can help me relax before the show. Just this once," he whispered. He pulled my arm forward until my face was next to his and he began kissing the side of it, and then my neck. His tongue was velvet. It wasn't like the boys I'd made out with before. It was magic.

I felt like I was in a trance, my body doing things my mind would never approve of. Soon I was laying down beside Edgar and I didn't care what I must look like to him. I wanted this as much as he did.

I closed my eyes, trying to imagine myself with the perfect body, like Georgina. He was touching me because I was beautiful and desirable. Not Edgar but Jack. He pushed his mouth hard against mine. I didn't want it to end. When the door flew open, I was yanked abruptly from my Georgina/Jack fantasy to the bed, with Edgar lying next to me. I opened my eyes and saw the panic on Edgar's face. Immediately I sat up, wanting this sudden nightmare to end.

"Gigi! Wait!" He pushed me over to the other side of the bed. It was already too late.

"I can't have this going down tonight. Not right before I perform. You should go after her!"

"I don't think that's a good idea." I was trying to take it all in, what I wanted, what had really happened, the horrible mixture of the two. "I'll talk to her on Monday. You should go warm up for your show." I didn't mean to be with Edgar. Maybe I enjoyed it. Yes, I enjoyed it. Maybe I felt like I was as good as Gigi for a few minutes.

"You're probably right. I should go warm up. I'll fix things with her later." He walked, naked and without shame, into the hall to get his pants.

Several people standing in the hallway made comments about his anatomy. "Lookin' good, Edgar!"

Chapter 7

Lois

I T HAD BEEN three months since that night. Gigi barely spoke to me. We never publicly argued, as so many girls did. Walking down the halls of Pepperville High was almost a better form of entertainment than television. Certainly more dramatic. But my former best friend and I pretended like we barely knew each other. It was as if we were two girls who hadn't shared secrets for so many years.

I began to notice that Gigi was dressing differently. Instead of the tight, form-fitting tops she normally wore, she was wearing flowery, flowing tops that looked like they came from the trash. The obvious snaps of Gigi's head away from my hopeful smiles were replaced by a vacant stare. It was like I was looking right through her.

One day after class, I followed her to the bathroom. I saw Gigi staring in the mirror. Her pants were partially unzipped. She wasn't enjoying her reflection, something she did almost weekly. "If you love yourself, everyone else will," she always told me when I caught her.

"Even your stomach is prettier than mine."

Gigi, startled, turned her back to me and began zipping her pants. "Go away."

"I'm sorry... I don't know why I did it. I just wanted to be you for one day. That's all it was. You can't imagine how hard it is to try and measure up to you."

Georgina drew her mouth in at the corners. "Edgar told me it didn't mean anything. That you seduced him."

It was so absurd. All of it. Did Edgar even know a word that complicated? I started laughing. I couldn't control myself and I bent over, chuckling so hard that tears started to flow from my eyes.

"Stop it! Why do you think this is funny? Am I going to have to beat you up?" Gigi challenged half-heartedly.

I stood up straight and wiped my eyes with the back of my hand. "I don't know how to seduce anyone. Can you think about that for a minute?"

Gigi smiled, the first smile she displayed publicly in months. "I guess you're right. When it comes to getting a guy interested, you suck."

I put my hands around my friend's waist. Strangely, I missed our intimacy as much as our conversation. "Can we just go back to being friends? I swear, I won't even look at Edgar again. Ever. It was a stupid mistake." *I once again find him repulsive.*

Gigi sighed. "I'm pregnant."

Chapter 8

Kenneth

"YOU HAVEN'T SEEMED like yourself for a while, is all I was saying," I closed my locker slowly. Lately, everything I said upset Georgina. Last week when I complimented her flowy green-and-purple top, she burst into tears. Right there in the middle of the hallway. Her skin was pasty and her hair, normally a luscious, wavy, chocolate brown work of art seemed like it was stuck to her head in viscous swirls and lumps.

"I know, Ken. You're trying to be nice. Things are kind of crazy right now, y'know?" Georgina looked like she was going to be sick for the third or fourth time that day; I'd lost track. She didn't know I kept track of that too.

"According to the book Lois found for me on this flu that's going around, I should only feel sick first thing in the morning, not all day. All my teachers are starting to get suspicious of all the bathroom passes I need. I hate not feeling normal."

"Can I walk you to Edgar's car? I could carry your books."

Normally she told me I was smothering her, but in her tired and weakened state, having someone else carry her books must have seemed like a pretty good idea. "Sure. Okay. I'm just walking home today though. Edgar has band practice. He's been rehearsing with Lost in Pepperville ever since the party several months ago... Well, you remember." She blushed. "They told him the bass player got high too often and forgot to show for performances so they needed a backup. I'm so happy for him." I took her books and juggled them under my arm with the two I was taking home. During the school year, I didn't get as much of a workout on the farm and my muscles just disappeared. Mom told me I needed to eat more of her special jam. There's only so much jam a boy can stomach in a week.

"I can walk you home if you want. My mom said she would be late today picking me up. She has to get groceries."

"Mildred always talks about rich people coming in to buy their groceries." Georgina shook her head. "She thinks they act like they're gracing her with their presence while they complain about the price of frozen Lima beans and load their carts with prime cuts of meat." She sighed. "Of course, we'll be eating noodles again at the Hardwick residence."

She stopped suddenly and pulled on my sleeve. I put my hand over hers, reveling in the softness of her skin.

"Tell me a story, Kenneth. I need to get my mind off my problems."

I rubbed her back for a minute while she bent over, looking like she was going to heave again.

"Well, you'll have to come out to our farm someday." She stood and motioned for me to continue walking. "It's like another world. Everything is so green and beautiful. You can see for miles when you sit on the ground above the potato cellar. We nicknamed it Spud Hill. It's a silence like you don't have in town. Can almost hear the grass grow. When harvest rolls around, the corn is tall and the fields just glisten."

Georgina snickered and then progressed to a full-blown chuckle. She continued until her eyes began to water. "Oh Kenneth, I'm sorry to laugh. It's just that you sound like a woman describing a soapy novel."

I shrugged. Half the time I didn't know what the heck she was talking about. It didn't matter. "Well, I suppose I sound a lot like my mom. I spend most of my time with her. You'd like her, I know it. Your mom—Mildred—probably never had a real conversation with her or she'd like her too."

"You're the only guy I know who brags about spending time with his mom." She smiled, forgetting momentarily about her physical issues.

"Okay, stop again for a minute. I need to close my eyes." Georgina put her hands at her temples and started rubbing. "This always helps. Give me a minute..."

"Gigi, I'm worried about you. This has been going on for a while. Do you need to see a doctor? Seems like it's more serious than the flu. You haven't been yourself since..."

"Since our hot and heavy night in Edgar's back seat? I know."

I looked away. It meant nothing to her. She was drunk and hurting. It meant everything to me. "Well, I was gonna say since you were crowned Homecoming Queen. That night you were upset too. Haven't seen you smile for months." I remembered that night, how I sat by myself in the row of chairs set up for the teachers. Edgar was so excited for her until he found out he wasn't crowned king. He stormed out before she finished her first dance with the king, Doake Browning. The twist of pain on her face was unbearable. I called Mom after that to come pick me up.

"I've only told Lois. And now you. Kenneth, I think I'm pregnant. No, I took a test, so I know for sure."

My jaw dropped. I began to calculate in my head, as best I could because these weren't things I knew much about from my studies of biology. "Gigi, is it true? You're having my baby!" It was almost too good to be true. Having a baby with the girl—no, woman—I loved.

She rolled her eyes. "I don't have the energy for this conversation. I didn't read the pamphlet that came with the pregnancy test, so I can't say for sure."

"You've got to tell your folks! You need to see a doctor, I'm pretty sure." I began walking quickly. "We should go tell your folks together. They need to know I'm not going to abandon you."

"Wait! Kenneth! Stop." Georgina paused, trying to catch her breath. "I haven't been able to eat an entire meal in several weeks and I'm always weak."

In my excitement, I was now several steps ahead of her. I turned around and came back to her side. "Oh,

Gigi. I'm sorry. Your condition. Should we sit down and rest for a few minutes?"

"No, Kenneth. Look, I have to figure out how to tell Edgar. He's going to freak. I need to figure things out with him before anything else. Can you keep this between us for now?"

I hiked the books up under my arm and reached around to hug her as a lump formed in my throat. "Of course. Poor Edgar. I won't tell anyone. I promise. We'll figure something out together."

We rounded the corner of Chesapeake to her house and stopped on the three concrete steps leading to her door. "Thanks, Kenneth. You're really cool." Georgina kissed me on the cheek.

I could smell the faint scent of vomit on her breath. "Don't worry about anything," I said, mentally listing all the potential problems ahead. I handed her books to her and walked down the steps, waving backward. "We'll figure this out together!"

She waved and smiled weakly. Even in her state of illness, she was the most beautiful person I had ever seen. Mom told me not to set my sights on someone who may not understand all my strengths. "Maybe you'll find someone who grabs your heart in some unlikely circumstance. You're still young." She was usually right about things, but this I knew for sure: Georgina was the only woman who would ever have my heart.

Chapter 9

Georgina

THEY WOULDN'T RESPOND well. The last time Mildred talked about someone getting pregnant without the benefit of marriage, she praised the parents who told the poor girl who would now be responsible for herself. "No room for that in a home with principles."

Lois offered to be with me when The Conversation happened, since Mildred always liked her. But even though we'd made up, I hadn't trusted her fully as a friend since I caught her with Edgar.

It was most important to tell Edgar. *What would he do?* I fantasized about him lifting me in the air, spinning me around and promising to make the three of us a happy family. We would move to San Francisco. Lots of women had babies and made their dreams come true. It was in Mildred's *True Woman Magazine*. I made a promise to myself, right there, that the next time I felt good I would tell Edgar about the baby.

The next morning turned out to be just such a day. I was clear-headed, well-rested, and maybe even a little happy. I took bright sunshine coming through the curtains onto my face as a good omen. Georgina Hardwick was ready to take on the world.

"You're eating breakfast today? I've been worried about this diet you've been on. You'll look just fine in your bathing suit even if you have a few meals," she commented as I inhaled two pieces of toast and a large bowl of sugar flakes. It felt good.

Mildred was always picking at the way I looked. When I developed before most of my classmates, she clucked her tongue and looked away every time I put on summer clothing. "You'd be better served by eating a bit less and dressing more sensibly. Keep yourself covered. You don't want to draw unnecessary attention."

I pulled on my winter coat and got the boys to school early, even kissing each one on the top of his head. "I'll see you after school, guys!" I called.

The boys waved and ran onto the playground. I was positive that today would be a good day.

Everything was starting off just as it should.

I waited by Edgar's locker until the bell rang, but he never came. We had fourth period Spanish together, and he came in ten minutes late with a note. Mr. Alifondo nodded. "Take your seat, Mr. Pepper."

Edgar winked as he sat next to me. I gently kicked his leg and he kicked mine in return. Our best communication was always in the form of something physical. After class, we walked together to lunch. "I've got to talk to you about something," I whispered in his ear.

"You're never gonna believe what happened to me this morning." Edgar squeezed my hand.

"Somebody started a fire at our implement dealership. Well, not somebody. It was Craig Balzine. He's only worked there for three weeks. He piled up a bunch of rags he used for cleaning equipment in the shop area. Dad always says they'll spontaneously combust. I thought that wasn't a real thing. Guess Dad knew what he was talking about. Sounds cool, right?"

"Oh no!" I faked interest, something I perfected in all aspects of my life. "Was anyone hurt?"

"Nah, just a lot of equipment damaged. But now my dad wants me to come work there for a while until he can find someone to replace Craig. I don't know how long after graduation I'll have to stay, but we might have to wait on our San Francisco plans."

I pulled his hand until he stopped. "That's what I wanted to talk to you about. Maybe it will be a good thing to wait a few months."

"Yeah, that's what I was thinking. We can go in the fall—"

"Edgar, I'm going to have your baby." I tilted my head to the side and smiled just slightly like I had seen in the movies hundreds of times.

"You sure?" His expression didn't change.

I put his hand on my belly. "Yeah. That's not food. It's a kid."

Edgar yanked his hand away quickly and looked around. "Don't do that in public. We don't want anyone else to know about this... just yet."

"I know it's crazy, right? I don't know what to think about it either, but, well, we've got to figure things out." I remember saying just that. I wondered for a moment if Kenneth felt as hurt by my response as I was by Edgar's.

We walked in silence to the courtyard. "Do you think it's a boy?" Edgar asked after we ate our sandwiches.

"Probably." I stared at the teacher parking lot. "Are we going to get married? I don't know if my parents will be too happy if we don't. People will talk."

"Of course. We have to. That's how things go. Hey– we can name our kid after our favorite rock group. Freaky Wings? That would be far out. Maybe

Dinasmith. What a cool kid's name that would be."
"Yeah!" I fake-smiled. "Cool."

That night at dinner, as I dished up a second helping of noodles and canned peaches, I thought about telling my parents.

"Family, I have the best news to share!" Dad took off his tie and threw it on the kitchen stool before bending down to kiss his wife on the top of the head.

"What is it, dear?"

"Well," he scooched his chair up to the table, "I may be getting a raise. They are going to expand the shoe store. The owners bought the old candy factory next door. You remember Dot's Vanilla Confections, dear?"

"Oh yes. My favorite as a child." Mildred took her husband's plate and heaped it with noodles.

"Well, they've decided to put a clothing store in half of the space and fill the other half with more shoes!"

"Yay! Daddy!" Brett clapped his hands and then unceremoniously smacked his brother in the face.

"Owie! Mom!" Calvin hit his brother back across the head. Mildred pulled Brett's chair back from the table because it was the closest one to her. "To your rooms, now!" The boys whined but eventually got down from the table and went to their rooms. On the nights Mildred felt the energy to discipline, they spent extra time throwing toys at their bedroom doors while in quarantine. It was a relief to eat in peace.

She turned and smiled at her husband. "Excellent news, Bob! We'll have to celebrate! I've been wanting to have your boss over for dinner some weekend anyway. They have some nice pork chops on sale at the Shoppe and Walke." Mildred patted her husband's arm and they gazed at each other lovingly.

"I have some news too," I said quietly.

"Oh?" Bob looked at me hopefully. "You're looking much better than you have in months. Other than the extreme amount of makeup that you know I disapprove of, you're looking like our girl again.

Whatever that bug was, it certainly hung on."

"Yeah. I..." I stared at my parents. They were smiling, holding hands. A rare moment when they weren't lost in the chaos of our home. "I'm going to start filling out college applications. I got one from the counselor today."

Mildred clapped her hands.

"The first Hardwick to go to college. I say we toast." Dad raised his glass of milk. "To our

Georgie, the first of her kind."

The next day at school, Kenneth stood in front of my locker, waiting patiently. I arrived just two minutes before class began. "Can you move it, Ken? I can't be late again." He moved only slightly, so I loaded his arms with my books for the day and used him as my personal book cart.

"I just wanted to tell you I'm sorry, but... I couldn't keep a secret from my mom. We tell each other everything. And I had to tell her about your... about our baby."

The color drained from my face. "You did what?"

"I told her. She's fine with it. Well, she wasn't happy that I, you know... had sex, but I'm growing up and it was bound to happen. That's what I said. But you can move in with us. We can get married and then we'll..."

"What? No, Kenneth. No. I'm not marrying you.

I'm marrying Edgar. He's my boyfriend."

"Gigi, you can't."

I slammed my locker door shut. "Don't tell me what I can or can't do. This is MY baby. I'll do whatever I want."

"That's not what's best for you. Edgar is... You deserve more..."

I stood uncomfortably close to Kenneth, bringing up memories of our night in the back seat. "I'm sorry I ever told you. I figured I could trust you and, clearly, you can't keep your mouth shut. In fact, I'm sorry I

60

slept with the most pathetic guy in the senior class when I could've had anyone."

The secretary came into my first-period class and whispered in my teacher's ear. I sat in the front row and leaned forward, trying to get any gossip I could to share with Edgar. "I was alarmed when I happened by the senior lockers. It was so out of character for him to be late for class. There he was, poor Kenneth Brownwell. He was sitting on the floor with his hat in his hand, his shirt soaked in tears. Broke my heart."

Chapter 10

Georgina

A WEEK WENT by without any more conversation about the pregnancy. I could feel my pants growing tighter, seemingly by the hour, and with that, my anxiety rose. Finally, I could take it no more. "Edgar, we need to tell our parents. They need to know we're not going to college first thing. And then the fact that we're going to San Francisco together with our... baby."

"You're right, babe. I've been working on something. I have a cousin who works at the courthouse. She told me you can get married at sixteen with parental consent. I kinda told her what was going on with us and she said she could sign the form for us, like a parent." Edgar smiled, proud he took charge of the situation. It would make his father proud.

"I guess."

For me, his plans seemed so formal, so final. It was much easier to think about San Francisco, that far-off and distant place where dreams came true.

Telling our parents was one thing, but actually doing something permanent, like getting married, was another. Sometimes, now that I was feeling better, I could pretend for a minute that this wasn't really happening. A new life growing inside me was a horrifying thought.

"This way we'll finish high school and then tell our parents," Edgar continued. "They can't say anything if we're already married. When we leave in the fall, things'll all be sorted out. You won't have the kid for a while, right?"

I still hadn't seen a doctor. Another thing that seemed like it would make all of this real. They were so gossipy at the doctor's office; that was the quickest way for my parents—as well as the rest of the neighborhood—to find out. Mildred talked about how Sissy, the lady at the front desk, would come in for groceries and gossip about everyone who came into the only clinic in town. *That Dawson boy? He's got a problem with his spine. He might have to have surgery and that will ruin his wrestling career.*

"I'm sure we've got some time. I guess it's probably good to get married. Like you said, nobody can make a fuss if it's already done." The words that came out of my mouth didn't match what I felt inside.

The following Friday, we left school at lunchtime and didn't go back. Edgar's cousin, Marybeth, signed the license in fancy curly handwriting for his mother and then plain, block-style letters for mine. "Do you have witnesses?" she asked. We looked at each other and shrugged. "That's okay, sometimes we just go down the hall to the probation office and see if anyone's checking in with their probation officer. They're always glad to have a diversion. Hold on." She soon returned with a habitual speeder named Tom and Loralee, the two-time shoplifter. After we exchanged vows, Tom and Loralee clapped. "Way to go, kids," Tom said jovially. "Me and my old lady have been together for over thirty years. You'll do just fine, long as you always talk things out." He offered a wrinkled hand.

Edgar shook his hand enthusiastically, as he was taught to do at the dealership when trying to show sincerity. "Thanks, man."

"I can't imagine... thirty years." I was half disgusted. That seemed too long to be with anyone.

Loralee patted me on the back. "Good luck, honey. You've got an uphill road at your age."

We left the courthouse with no rings, no ceremony, and only a piece of paper changing our status from single to married.

"Now what should we do?" Edgar asked. "My brothers both got a hotel room on their wedding night."

I rolled my eyes. "We can have sex any time. Can we drive out to the used clothing store on the highway first?"

I mulled over this strange new title, "Mrs. Edgar Pepper", as we drove. I rolled down the window and let the wind push my hair away from my face. Should I start calling my husband "dear" like Mildred and Bob did? Did we need to act differently? Nothing about this felt normal.

We drove two miles from downtown Pepperville to

Dori's Second Hand. After walking through a maze of wind chimes and antique gardening tools, we found the second-hand clothing section in the back. I picked out some large jeans and several tops and took them to the cash register where a woman with long, braided grey hair stood. She was just the type of person Mildred would hate; she was wearing a colorful, tie-dyed shirt with a peace symbol on a long chain around her neck and didn't appear to have bathed in a while. Mildred always called people who looked like this "dirty, hippy-dippy types". She stared at us.

"Can we check out, please?" I snapped.

"Peace, man. Just studying your auras. I'm pretty perceptive. You two just got married?"

We looked at each other in shock. "Yeah, why?" Edgar asked.

"I have a gift." She looked at the size tag in the jeans and then looked at me. "You know, I can help you make something work in your size. Most pregnant girls have some kind of panel sewed in, so it grows with their stomach. I'd be happy to do that for you."

I blushed. "Oh, I'm not..." I looked out the window. "Ok, yeah. I guess that would be good. How long would that take?"

"Come back a week from today. I'll find a couple more pairs of pants to fix up for you. Make you feel more normal wearing clothes that fit. It'll be okay, honey."

Tears slipped out of my eyes. "I'm sorry. That just happens for no reason." I sniffed, looking around for something to wipe my nose with.

"Here." Dori handed me a tie-dyed handkerchief

from one of the sale racks. "Nobody buys these anyway." She patted my back. "Can I read your palm?"

Edgar pulled on my sleeve.

"Ok," I replied, ignoring Edgar's insistent tugging.

The braided lady took my hands and squeezed them for a moment before turning them over to see the palms.

"Long lifeline. That's good. I see more than one child. And lots of struggles ahead. Something about red hearts... and the color purple. That's where you want to put your energy. It'll get you through. Does that mean anything to you?" I shook my head.

"Gigi, let's go," Edgar said, inching toward the door.

Dori held my hands tight. "As long as you're open to good people, good things will come your way. Can you remember that?"

"I'll remember."

Although Edgar was insistent, I convinced him we couldn't go to a hotel because I still had to babysit after school and he had to work at the dealership. The following week, we returned and picked up the pants– "maternity wear" as Dori called it. Edgar insisted on waiting in the car. "Hurry, Gigi.

That lady's nuts. Don't let her get in your head." I nodded.

Dori greeted me warmly and handed me the pants to try on. "Bathroom's back there, across from Buddha incense holder. Try them on and make sure I got it all right."

As I pulled the pants up over my raised belly, I felt comfortable for the first time. No more trying to squeeze all of myself into the jeans I so proudly purchased last year with babysitting money.

"Things are going to be rough for you, honey." Dori put the pants in a bag. "I can see lots of rough waters, like I said. Just keep your focus on those red hearts. And that boy in the car? He's not the one for you."

I looked at her with horror. "He's my husband!" Surely people didn't say that to married couples over twenty. I snapped my purse shut.

Dori shrugged. "I see what I see."

I took the pants home and shoved the bag in the farthest corner of my closet, hoping I wouldn't need them for a while. The usual dinner consisting of noodles, unruly six-year-olds, and my parents talking about their workdays seemed strange. If they really loved me, they would have noticed something drastically different with their only daughter. Instead, they acted as though it were any other evening.

There was another party at Lecher Farm on Saturday. Edgar was playing with Lost in Pepperville once more. "You gonna be there, babe? I mean, my old lady should always be watching."

I remembered the last party. Leaving Edgar alone all night didn't seem like the smartest choice. "Maybe. I probably shouldn't drink anymore though." I was seriously thinking about going to the doctor soon. Whenever I told my parents.

"I was thinking... maybe we could go to a hotel after. Like we planned to do the night we got married."

My heart melted. The fact that he hadn't forgotten reinforced what he had told me—the lady at the secondhand store didn't know anything. "Oh, Edgar. That's so romantic. But how would I?"

"Tell your parents you're staying with Lois. I'll tell mine I'm staying with somebody too. Just make sure Lois knows so if they call her she'll cover for you."

Lois owed me this one. Even though I didn't trust her friendship, it was a safe bet she felt guilty enough to agree to anything. At least she hadn't told anyone about the baby. "Okay. Let's do it."

I saw Lois at the party, talking to a sophomore who routinely followed me around the school all year. I always ignored him. When Lois recognized my face, she ran across the room. "Gigi! I'm glad you called, even if it was only about giving you an alibi. We need to go do something together! Maybe next weekend?"

"Yeah, sure." I no longer needed Lois in my life, beyond Edgar's and my secret outings. We would be leaving eventually and we would make new friends in San Francisco. I didn't plan on keeping in touch with anyone from here.

By the time Edgar finished his set, I'd been sitting in the kitchen for almost an hour, my feet propped up on a red-and-black stool. Though I hadn't told anyone else and no one said anything, I assumed most people already heard the rumor about my pregnancy.

We drove in silence to the motel, where I undressed under the covers and waited for Edgar to come out of the bathroom. His eyes were bloodshot and he smelled like pot. He crawled in beside me, his taut body sending the normal shivers down my spine. He caressed my body until he got to my stomach. He pulled his hand away abruptly.

"That's weird. Sorry, but that's weird. Thinking about a kid in there. Like an alien or something, you know?"

He laid back, putting his hands behind his head. "You should hear the song playing in my head right now. It's something new I'm gonna write. About becoming famous at eighteen."

I sighed. "I'm tired." I rolled over and turned out the light.

The next morning, Edgar dropped me off on Chesapeake Street. I felt relieved to be away from him. I had to admit the thought of spending every day together seemed challenging, at least until we were in a big city where there were many distractions.

I tromped up to my bedroom, ready to get out of my tight clothes and maybe into my pajamas. I was surprised to see my parents sitting on my bed. Mildred was holding the bag of maternity pants on her lap. Her eyes were red-rimmed. Bob was sitting, legs crossed, his hands folded and resting on top of them.

"We called Lois's house. She said you'd be home an hour ago. I guess you've got worse secrets than that." Mildred sniffed. "How could you?" She held up the pants. "We have given you everything. All we asked was that you behave in an appropriate fashion. You've betrayed your family."

"It's probably the rock music and tight clothing. We've talked about this before, Mildred. We should have taken the problem seriously a year ago."

"I... why were you in my closet? That's my private space!" It was all happening too quickly. I grabbed the sack out of my mother's hands. "Can't I have any privacy?"

"We found a leak in the kitchen yesterday. We had to find out where it was coming from before calling a plumber. When I looked through your closet for moisture," Mildred pointed to the bag, her voice wavering, "I found this. Clothing for a... Oh, Georgie. We raised you to be a good girl." She began to sob.

My face turned bright red. I had no time to come up with a good story. "I AM a good girl. I've already gotten married. You didn't ask, but the father is Edgar. He and I went down and got married on our own."

Mildred put her hand on her chest. "Oh, Lord. I can't believe it. You went and married a boy? On your own? How did you do it without our permission?"

"Wait a minute, dear. I need to know—is this the young man you've been seeing? His family owns the implement dealership?"

I nodded. "And I married him." I was proud that Edgar and I were mature enough to handle things on our own.

"Well, then you shouldn't be living under our roof." Mildred hopped down from the bed and put her hands on her small hips. "A married woman lives with her husband. And you'll quit school immediately. It's not acceptable for a young woman in your 'state' to be causing a stir in public. Oh, Bob, how will we deal with the neighbors?"

Dad stood and looked sternly at me. "Your mother is right. You need to move in with your husband immediately. We'll need to contact the boy's parents and find a suitable place for you to live." He turned to leave the room.

"Wait!" Things were playing out as if we were watching an old movie on television, except there were no commercials to slow down the action. My entire world had changed, and I'd only been in the house a few minutes. "We're planning to move. To San Francisco. Maybe I could just stay here until school is done and then we'll leave together."

Mildred laughed. "Oh, Georgie, you're not going anywhere. You'll be consumed by your child. The sooner you get used to it, the better. Life as you know it is over."

My parents walked out of the room, continuing the conversation in earshot. "At least the boy comes from a respectable home," Mildred remarked.

After a tense five days, where there was no unnecessary conversation in the house, I babysat my brothers while my parents met with Edgar's parents. They came home, somber faced, and asked the boys to play in their room.

"You'll be moving into an apartment with your husband next week. The Peppers are making arrangements. They've recently remodeled The Pepperville Arms and you'll have adequate living accommodations there," Dad said matter-of-factly. "Your mother and I will take care of notifying the school and our employers. It's best that we attack this before rumors get out of hand."

I began to cry. This lump inside of me was

destroying my life. "I don't want to quit school!" I sobbed.

"You should have thought of that long ago." Mildred drew the corners of her mouth together. "Oh, Bob, I didn't think about the boys. What will we do with the boys after school? They can't stay by themselves."

"I can still take care of them! I'll come over and I'll..."

"No." Mildred shook her head vigorously. "That wouldn't be proper. They're too young to be exposed. You'll not tell them anything."

When I went back to school on Monday, I brought a note from my parents, explaining my situation and that I would be quitting school by the end of the week. Most of my teachers looked at me with pity but said nothing. My geometry teacher clucked her tongue. "Such a waste."

I never looked Kenneth in the eye. A couple of times he tried to talk to me, but I refused. I couldn't bear his looks of pity and understanding. Especially after how I'd treated him. On my last day, Lois came up to me and handed me a crumpled piece of paper. "This is Kenneth's phone number. He asked me to give it to you. In case you're ever in trouble."

I cried as I packed up my room. All my stuffed animals, albums, and the posters I'd pulled from teen magazines; all of it went into boxes to take to this new life I hadn't asked for. Mildred came in only once, holding a small, empty box. "I just thought you might want to box up your camera and leave it for the boys. I can make sure they don't use it until they're old enough to do so responsibly."

How could my mother be so dismissive? Suddenly I wasn't even a member of her family. "I'm still going to San Francisco," I said defiantly. "I'll be taking my camera with me."

"I don't know what you're talking about. You'll hardly have the energy to put on clean clothes. I doubt you'll be taking any car trips."

My hatred for her grew by the minute. She never supported me. I was never anything more than a babysitter for her.

By Friday, I was disconnected from everything that was familiar. My room, formerly full of life and noise, was an empty space with four bright pink walls.

"Why do you always cry?" Brett asked as they sat on the couch, watching cartoons.

"Because I'm moving. That makes me sad." I tried holding the tears back, but every day it became harder. Now I seemed to cry all the time.

"Mom said you had to move when you did something bad. Will you ever come back?" He and his brother put their heads on my shoulders.

"Maybe." I put my arms around each boy and hugged them tightly. For once, they didn't squirm.

My parents helped take the boxes into the upstairs apartment, something extremely challenging for Mildred's four-foot-ten-inch frame. The emotion of the last week had been almost more than I could bear. I wanted to curl up in a corner, but I knew it was important to keep working as long as my parents were critiquing my every move. If I stopped, they would decide I was being lazy and they wouldn't continue helping. Mildred walked slowly to the living room, where I was unpacking the brown-swirled plates Edgar's parents had donated to us. She tapped me on the back.

I turned to stare at my mother, noting her eyes were red-rimmed as if she'd spent time out of sight crying. "Are you going?" I forced a smile, hoping she might take the hint and offer a hug. When Mildred didn't budge, I stood up and hugged her stiff body. "I'll miss you," I said quietly.

Mildred pulled away from my embrace. "You've really put us in a bind with the boys. Someday you'll understand the mess you've created, but by then you will have wasted your entire life." She shook her head, the way she did when someone she disliked was in the Shoppe and Walke.

I swallowed my emotions. "Thank you for helping with the move."

"I suppose this is it," Bob said, gazing in disgust at the inordinate number of orange blobs on the wallpaper. "I wish you the best." He shook Edgar's hand, the first formal communication between my father and husband. Bob nodded somberly toward me before walking out the door.

After Edgar and I were alone into our two-bedroom apartment, the scent of fresh paint still hanging in the air, we sat on our orange, nylon-loop couch and stared at each other. We'd never actually been in a home together. I realized our entire relationship before today had taken place in a car or at a party. "What do we do now?" he asked. "I know how to cook noodles."

Chapter 11

Georgina

I T WAS BECOMING increasingly uncomfortable to do anything. I felt huge and awkward, though I wasn't sure how far along I was. Going to the doctor where everyone would stare would be too embarrassing. The doctor would look at my age, shake his head, and then talk about the pregnant high school girl to all of his nurses. I felt enough judgment already.

Things with Edgar were uncomfortable too. As a couple, we usually only spent a few hours a day together. Since he stayed up late practicing his guitar, I painstakingly applied all my makeup and then posed myself in the bed. I splayed my hair out on the pillow, the way models did in Mildred's *Weekly Journal* magazine ads. I wanted him to desire me as much as he had when we stole time together in the back seat of his car. Instead, Edgar flipped the light off when he came into the room and went to bed without acknowledging my presence.

"We should dress in the bathroom, so we don't have to... you know, see each other," I announced at breakfast one morning. All the information I obtained about married life came from articles in *True Woman Magazine*, such as "Keep the Mystery Alive in Your Marriage."

"Mmhmm..." Edgar was reading the court records portion of the *Pepperville Daily Times* to make sure no one from the band had been arrested.

I was embarrassed about the way my body was changing. I didn't know what normal was, and I knew my husband got all his information about women's bodies from his father's X-rated magazines.

"We can keep the mystery alive, right?"

"What?" Edgar looked at me and then turned away. He was barely able to meet my gaze anymore.

I knew he realized my face was getting puffier.

I sighed. "Never mind."

After he left for the day, I was stuck at home, trying to find things to do. We didn't have many baby things, though I wasn't that interested. The extra room sat empty, other than the boxes of albums and a few of the boys' newborn outfits Mildred had placed in my box of underwear without telling me.

I missed the politics of senior year and the friends who came and went from my locker. I missed all the boys staring at me longingly. There were only so many soap operas I could watch and beauty magazines I could read.

One day, on impulse, I picked up the phone and dialed Lois's number.

"Hello?" It was Lois's mother.

"This is Georgina Hardwick. Georgina Pepper, actually. I was just wondering if Lois was busy?"

There was a long pause. "We've heard about your

unfortunate situation. I told Lois she isn't to speak to you anymore. You're not exactly the type of person I want around my daughter. I'm sure you understand." She hung up before I could respond. I'd wondered why Lois hadn't stopped by. It was a blow to think she no longer needed me. Her mother covered for me all those times without question.

When Edgar came home that night, I relived the entire gut-wrenching conversation for him.

He banged his fist on the table. "Screw them all. Sometimes people come into the dealership and stare at me. I know what they're thinking. 'Poor stupid kids.' They don't know we're going to leave this all behind. We'll be out of here before you know it. Since Dad gave us this place rent free for a whole year, it won't take long at all." He looked out the window at the cars driving into the parking lot. "Don't worry, Gigi. I've got this."

"Thanks, dear!" I came over and attempted to hug him from behind. He jerked away. I began to sob, hard long sobs. I hadn't cried in days and it was overdue. I reached for the back of the chair so I didn't fall forward.

"I miss being touched," I blurted. I wanted him to understand this ache of loneliness. The feeling of being tossed away. But nothing I said or did ever seemed to get through. "I feel like... I feel like some sort of freak. Nobody will talk to me. You act like I'm contagious. I don't think this is how marriage is supposed to be."

Edgar squinted. "You think this is hard? I have to work all day. I'm bored out of my mind. I'd love to just sit here all day and watch TV like you do. Instead, my brothers laugh at me and my dad doesn't think I know what I'm doing. My life is ten times harder than yours."

I was sobbing so hard the neighbors began to bang on the wall. Edgar looked at me with pity or disgust, I wasn't good at telling the difference anymore.

"This isn't... I mean... I'm not good at these things. Maybe you should get a stuffed animal or something." He grabbed his coat. "I'm going to practice with the band. Probably not a good idea for us to have an argument in your condition."

"Wait! Please don't go!" Edgar didn't stop moving. He was out the door before I could say anything else. I was out of tears. Empty. I sat down in the middle of the living room floor, staring at the orange blobs on the wallpaper and the fancy knickknacks Edgar's mother carefully placed on the shelves. There was nothing that felt familiar. Nothing that said I lived there. It struck me that decorating might be the one thing to entice my mother to come to visit. We could move things to her level.

I picked up the phone and dialed her number. "Hardwick Residence, Brett speaking."

Our last cuddle on the couch was just a few weeks old, but I missed the boys already. My voice trembled. "You're answering the phone like such a big boy! I miss you!"

There was a muffled conversation on the other end. "Georgina?" It was Mildred. "Is that you?"

"It's me, Mom. I've missed you. I wanted to know if you were interested in coming over. Maybe we could have tea or something? I know you like tea. I've been thinking about how to decorate and you're always so good at that."

There was an awkward moment of silence. Foolishly, I hoped she was thinking about how much she missed my presence at the dinner table.

"We made our position very clear. We don't approve of the choices you've made and now you'll face the consequences. Your father told you we don't want any further contact." The line clicked and then went dead.

Just like that, Mildred could end our lives together. I felt like an old dishrag, used up and thrown away. I was just a glorified babysitter for the twins. I was never their daughter. My mother pretended to like me every once in a while, but it had been a ruse. It was as much and as little as I could expect from Mildred Hardwick.

I hung the phone up on the wall and blew my nose, disgusted that there was an endless supply of tears for the events in my life. "Pull yourself together, Georgina," I said. I looked around at the boxes. Maybe I could decorate on my own. Edgar's father gave us a substantial monthly allowance for anything we might need.

I began searching for my camera. I could take pictures and frame them to hang on the walls as practice. I opened a box of my closet items and then another, finally finding the camera in with my school supplies. There was a wadded-up piece of paper at the bottom of the box, which I picked up to read. It was the paper that Lois handed me on my last day of school. I uncrumpled it to see the perfectly square blocks of lettering that read, "Kenneth Brownwell, phone, 272-4400, address, 61 Brownwell Lane." I smiled, thinking about his serious, perfect world.

I picked up the phone and dialed but then hung up. There was enough rejection already today. How could I handle things if the one person who worshipped me rejected me as well?

That night I skipped makeup and just turned out the light and went to sleep. It wasn't worth it, waiting up for Edgar. Nothing would come of it anyway.

The next day, I sorted through boxes again. I found my school binder, the one a silly teen girl covered with *Mrs. Edgar Pepper* in various swirly letters. Now that it was real, it no longer seemed like an identity I wanted.

On the back of the binder was the yearly Pepperville High School calendar, something taped there with a bit of irritation so many lifetimes ago. It was parent-teacher conference week, something viewed as an extra holiday for those with good grades. Now it felt like a stab in the chest, that I was no longer good enough to be a part of something that was so meaningless before.

Every single person my age was out of school. I decided to take my camera and walk to Main Street, where everyone would either cruise or hang out on their day off. As I rounded the corner, I noticed three girls from my class sitting on the park bench, giggling and sharing a bottle of Grape-a-licious.

"Gigi!" Shelly squealed. "We've missed you." She ran over and hugged me tightly. I held on for several seconds, relishing her touch. Shelly pulled away and looked at my belly. "Wow, you're getting big."

The other two girls came over and stood beside me, looking around at the cars passing and honking. "You're like the plague. Every parent in town has warned us away from you," Shelly commented sarcastically.

"We even had a school assembly about keeping our pants on. 'Don't talk about it, don't think about it,'" Mara, the only girl in their class almost as tall as me added. "Don't touch unless it's a handshake," the other two chimed in. All three girls giggled nervously.

"Yeah. I can imagine. You guys want to come over to my place? I'm trying to decorate, but I could use some ideas. It's only a couple of blocks away." I put my hand in front of my eyes ostensibly to shield them from the sun, but also to avoid their stares.

"We've got, um..." Shelly stuttered.

"We're waiting for people. We really can't, but thanks," Mara finished. I displayed the same look of disapproval a thousand times when people of lesser status expected me to socialize with them.

"If you change your mind, I could give you my address." I felt stupid as soon as I said it. There was no way they were coming over. I wished I was still the popular girl I was the last time I saw them. They wouldn't have dared treat me like this.

"Maybe next time, 'kay?" Shelly turned and pulled on Mara's elbow. All three girls walked away and were still within earshot when they started whispering about me.

I clenched my jaw tight for a moment and then took in a large breath. "I'm not going to cry," I said, hoping they would hear me. They were already across the street, talking to some boys from our class who stopped to flirt. I took a picture of them laughing and throwing their heads back like they didn't have a care in the world. A sudden spark of defiance overtook me. I decided to walk around the entire square that was Main Street.

I walked into Flowers, Flowers, and Fudge on a whim.

Lois was working at the counter, her thin hair pulled tightly in a bun, the style I'd reminded her several times made her head look like a misshapen eraser.

"Hi, Lois! I miss your pinkie!" I said cheerfully.

She looked up from her paperwork. Her face reminded me of a wax figure in a museum, if that face were grey in tone.

"Hi... um... what are you doing here?"

"Just hungry for fudge. What do you recommend?" Lois knew I hated fudge. Our joke was that when she wanted to get rid of me, she would show up at our door with a tray of Pepperville Peppermint.

Lois looked to the back of the store. "My mom will be back soon," she whispered. "She doesn't want me talking to you."

"You can't sneak out sometime after school and just say hi? What would that hurt?" I hated that I was so needy.

"I'm not going to lie to my mom. I'm not like you." She smirked.

"Well, I guess we're done then. That was a waste of a friendship." I thought my tears had reached their limit. I was wrong. Her stare burned a hole in my back as I stormed out.

When I was a freshman, there was a sophomore girl

who became pregnant by a freshman boy. It was scandalous until the principal called her parents and told them she needed to quit school instead of disrupting everyone's studies. I never saw her again. Today I wished I could remember her last name so I could go to her home and apologize for making fun of her.

I halfheartedly took a photo of Dante's Levels of Couches but continued on. I found myself in front of the Shoppe and Walke, peering through the large letters painted on the window: *Pot Roast 79 cents per pound this week only!*

I took a picture of Mildred standing on her box at the checkout. Something in me felt excited to see her, no matter how she treated me. I could read the "disgusted with wild youth running free" look on her face. I stood, defiantly, in front of the window.

The wife of the car shop repairman, Mrs. Sheldon, was buying several cartons of wafer cookies and fresh carrots. Mildred was standing on her box, laughing as she typed the price of each item into the cash register. I could hear her voice but couldn't quite make out the words no matter how hard I strained to hear. I raised the camera to my eye and snapped a picture, as close as I could, of Mildred's conversational smile.

When Mrs. Sheldon finished, she took her bag and then the pleasant look on her face tightened. She touched Mildred's sleeve and pointed to the window.

Mildred's smile dissolved into a stony look of disapproval. She shook her head and then got off her box and left the front of the store. My heart fell. I noticed my reflection in the window between the large painted letters. I was very round – bigger than I ever imagined I would be. Pregnant women in *True Woman Magazine* were stylish and thin. That *thing* inside of me was taking over and ruining everything.

I hurried home, to the anonymity of the orange blob-covered walls. The camera went into a box of my best clothes. I found Kenneth's number and dialed it once more.

"Can I speak to Kenneth? This is a friend of his from school." There was no way I would make the mistake of giving my name again.

"Oh? A friend?" There was uncontained glee on the other end. "Wait just a minute and I'll get him." The phone dropped on the counter and I heard, "Kenneth! Ken! It's a friend, honey! You've got a friend on the phone!"

There was some rattling and then he picked up. "Hel-lo?" he said suspiciously. "Who is this?"

"It's just me. Gigi."

"OH!" There was a muffled conversation on the other end. "I'm going into the study. Can you hold on?"

There was heavy breathing on the other end and then, "Ok, Mom, I've got it." He paused a moment before continuing, "I've missed seeing your beautiful face, Gigi. How are you doing?"

The corny words that once would have made me cringe melted my heart in this moment. "Kenneth, I've really missed you too. I'm so sorry for the way I treated you. I was going through a lot and shouldn't have taken it out on you."

"Oh heck, Gigi. Don't apologize. Mom explained things. You have a lot of changes... things a simple guy like me wouldn't understand. I shouldn't have been so forward."

We talked for almost an hour about everything and everyone I hadn't seen since my life became about blob-covered walls and a distant husband. I kept finding silly new topics just to keep his voice on the line. Just to feel normal.

"I'm sorry, but I've gotta go. I have chores I have to do. I promised my mom I would get them done before sundown, and these days that's pretty early."

"Oh." My voice dropped. I would be alone again, waiting for another awkward conversation with Edgar. "Can you call me back? Maybe tomorrow?"

"Yeah!" Kenneth's excitement was obvious. "No problem! I'll call you tomorrow. Same time?"

I sighed. "Any time. I'm not doing anything at all."

"Okay. I'll call you back tomorrow after I do my chores. And Gigi? The offer still stands: you can always come here."

Chapter 12

Frannie

I MAKE IT my business to know everything that goes on in this town. Everything. Other women with money use it to get their hair or nails done. I use mine to pay for information because I hate surprises, especially when they involve my Ken.

I knew Edgar's story before I knew his face. He was the third of three boys born to Franklin and Edwina Pepper. The family's implement dealership was the largest building in Pepperville, sitting just on the outskirts of town. His mother, Edwina, was a serious, sturdy woman with short grey hair, cat-eye glasses, and a large mole in the middle of her forehead. She always made it seem as though her boys were better than everyone else. They were naturally strong with wide, sturdy faces and darker skin that Edwina said came from a Cherokee great-great-grandfather.

Each boy was expected to work in the dealership like their father, enjoy sports, and marry a girl from a proper family. The older two boys (Franklin Jr. and Ned) married sisters (Shorla and Mya) from the Shedley family who owned a large, productive pig farm. The lavish weddings cost each family around $15,000, the proper amount for a respectable ceremony in Edwina's eyes.

Franklin, a forty-six-year-old former star quarterback for the Fighting Soybeans told his son he was disappointed when Edgar decided not to go out for football. He understood that he didn't want to do track because it interfered with planting season, the busiest time of year at the dealership. But the one thing he struggled to tolerate was Edgar's love of music.

Edgar never argued with his father. It was pointless. Franklin was always right, even when he wasn't. Sometimes Edgar's sister-in-law Shorla would allow him to practice his used guitar at their home if she was out getting her nails done. In the evenings, he put the guitar in his lap and placed his hands just above the strings, pretending to strum.

His elderly neighbor liked to watch him, especially when Edgar was roaming around without wearing his shirt. She possessed a keen interest in the Pepper family and often listened at the windows, left open year-round to encourage robust blood flow. She wrote down every conversation that took place at the Pepper house, supplying any details to not just me but anyone who asked.

When Edgar passed most of his classes junior year, Franklin was forced to buy his son the ThreeTone Sunburst Electric Thorton that sat in the display window of Reekblast Rimshots for two years. He made the boy promise he would never plug it in while his parents were home.

"Don't play that thing while I'm home," Franklin reminded his son, likely regretting the day he agreed to the purchase of the most expensive guitar available in Pepperville. "Your time should be focused on things that matter."

Pathetic Edgar often sat in his car and strummed even though there was no sound coming out. The neighbor, who by now had purchased binoculars expensive, reported that Edgar gave the impression he decided he was getting good. Soon he would have regular gigs where underage kids weren't drinking, and he would invite his parents to watch. That's when he would tell them about the move to San Francisco.

They knew about Georgina. She wasn't from a wealthy family, but she was stunning. As long as she had that going for her, she would make an acceptable hostess for the monthly customer appreciation nights at Pepper Implement-Ville.

"Dad, I gotta tell you something." Edgar caught his father after the sale of two of their most expensive combines.

Franklin gulped his third vodka of the night. "What is it, son?"

"Well..." Edgar looked at the gold carpet. Even though his father's eyes were glassy, Edgar couldn't stand looking him in the eye. "Georgina. She's gonna have a baby."

Franklin sat up straight. "You sure it's yours?"

It probably never occurred to Edgar that Georgina would cheat. Girls didn't do that. "Yeah, it's mine."

"Well then, we've got to make this legitimate. Your mother will want to plan a wedding. It'll have to be quick, but I can pull together something. Probably no more than one hundred, mostly the muckety-mucks. You know how your mother enjoys that. We'll need to speak to the girl's parents."

"Could you tell Mom?" The only thing Edgar feared more than telling his father was his mother's reaction. She scared most of the folks around town.

Franklin nodded. He held out his empty glass. "Pour me another one and I'll break it to her the best I can."

"Dad? You don't have to worry. We already got married."

Franklin shook his head. "Better you told me first, son."

Edwina sobbed for several days, at the same time refusing any conversation with Edgar. The fact that her baby was marrying beneath him was less important than the fact she didn't get to plan his wedding. That's what she told her hairdresser, and you don't lie to a hairdresser.

When she was finally able to bring herself to talk to her son, she waited patiently by the front door. As soon as he came in and dropped his books on the couch, she caught him from behind, pulling his ear like she had done publicly when he was little.

"To the kitchen," she said firmly.

Edgar knew resisting was futile.

She pulled his ear until he was in the sitting position at the table. "You listen to me, son. Your father and I were forced to sit with those circus freaks and listen to them judge us. I was stuck trying to smile while that woman told me about how her daughter was Little Miss Perfect until you corrupted her. Made me sick to my stomach."

Edgar refused to cry. No matter how Edwina tried to break him, he hadn't cried since he was a child; when she made him sit facing the wall while the rest of the family ate dinner and long after, until his father went to bed. She often bragged she made him a man that day.

"It doesn't matter to me that you got your tramp girlfriend pregnant. Both of your sisters-in-law were pregnant when they got married. But I'm not going to deal with that family again. Smug trash. You teach the idiot how to be a good Pepper and maybe I'll let the kid come to visit at Christmas. Understood?" Edgar nodded.

That night his father came into his bedroom without knocking. Edgar tried to hide his guitar but he wasn't quick enough. "Sorry, Dad, I wasn't playing."

"It's all right." He sat down on his son's bed. "I just need to let you know what I've decided."

Edgar slid his guitar under his bed. "Okay."

"We're going to move you and Georgina into the new apartment building. You can have the biggest unit; I haven't rented it out yet. Your mother can decorate it. That will make up for the wedding she missed."

Edgar shrugged.

"You'll have to start working at the dealership full time right away. Your brothers had better timing." He winked. "At least they waited until they were done with school."

"I don't want to work there full time. Can't I just go in a couple of days a week?"

"No, son. This is how things work. You'll get used to it after a while. I give incentives for big sales months. Maybe you'll hit that and get yourself a nice big bonus check."

Edgar showed little interest in school. He was more focused on getting out of town, where he planned on chasing his dream. I believe he always planned to leave town without Georgina. The idea of him wanting to take a baby on that adventure just hits me wrong.

Edwina spent many days with her decorator and her maid (also a convenient informant for me) perfecting the look of the apartment. The baby blue appliances were transported by truck from Des Moines and almost didn't make it in the time she allotted. When she threatened to come to the appliance store personally and break anything expensive, a truck went out immediately. In addition to the three-tone, orange-flowered wallpaper, she put up a little shelf with decorations she had been keeping in a box for Edgar's first home with the wife of her choosing. Her prized, tiny 3D Japanese garden in a glass front box sat prominently in front of Edgar's grade school pictures. "Don't let your wife dust that. I'll come over and take care of it myself," she warned. She took Edgar through the apartment with the maid the day before Georgina was to move in so she could avoid any kind of communication misconstrued as friendly between herself and Georgina's parents.

"I think I've outdone myself." She looked around with satisfaction and folded her arms in front of her. "You can come for dinner sometime soon."

Edgar tried to hug her goodbye, but she slapped his arm aside. "There'll be none of that. Don't think I approve of your stupid decision. We were planning on your marrying Holly Genders. Now she'll be wasted on some moron from the power plant."

He nodded. He dated Holly for two months until Holly told him she didn't really like guys.

When Georgina's parents moved her in and left, he stared at his new bride with a newfound discomfort. Their conversations had always been about parties and people who did dumb things in school. "I'm gonna practice my guitar," he said, trying to avoid his wife's intense stare.

It felt strange, living with someone in his space. Georgina's eyes were always swollen from crying, and he didn't want to ask what was upsetting her. He didn't know how to handle those things.

The worst part was that she was so clingy. One of the things that made her most attractive to him was the fact that she was strong and independent. Like his mother. Now she was a weepy mess, always wanting to be held or comforted. He told this story over prime rib at his parents' house three days later. The maid was disgusted; she felt so bad, she showed up unannounced at the apartment with leftover meat and homemade bread. She set the table, wanting to say something but knowing it wasn't her place to interfere.

"Edgar, will you rub my feet? They hurt so much."

He'd experienced a hard day of sales, trying to pretend like he understood each piece of equipment. He didn't care what each tractor did in the field. The last thing he wanted was to take care of someone else.

"Not tonight. I'm going to practice my guitar. You gonna eat this? I'm not much for leftovers. No offense, Felida."

Felida shrugged. Her boss wouldn't be happy knowing she shared something from their refrigerator with Edgar's new bride.

Georgina shook her head. "I ate crackers all day."

"You told me you were going to go through those cookbooks my mom put in the cupboards. It can't be that hard."

Georgina began to cry again. "Then I would have to go to the store. My mom's day off isn't until Thursday. I can't go while she's there, or..."

Edgar sighed. "I know. You don't want her to make fun of you or whatever. Maybe I'll get a burger then." He picked up his keys. "I'll see you later."

Felida knew he would be welcomed at his parents' house, eating whatever was on the menu for this evening. His mother seemed to relish the fact that Georgina was failing in all aspects of domesticity.

As the days drug on, one thing became increasingly clear: marriage wasn't what either of them wanted. He brought it up often but scoffed when she wanted to talk about her aches and pains instead. Later, she confessed their last night together was the epitome of their struggles.

He started out seeming as though he was going out

of his way to be nice. He acknowledged that she was right, he hadn't wanted to touch her. "Gigi, we haven't had... you know... since we moved in together. If I promise to close my eyes, do you think we might?"

"You think that makes me want to jump in bed with you? You are clueless, man. Totally clueless." She thought she might have reached the point where she couldn't feel the sting of rejection anymore. She was wrong. Gigi went into the bathroom and slammed the door shut.

"Gigi?" Edgar knocked at the door several times without response. "Everyone at work is older and makes fun of everything I say. Whenever I have a bad day, they say, 'Try being married for twenty years. Poor baby.' And my parents... they only want to hear about the bad stuff you do. It's just really hard. Guess I wanted you to know that. Bein' me isn't as easy as it sounds."

She didn't reply. There was nothing she could say because he wasn't the listening type. Later that night, he went to practice with his band. Those young people didn't take much encouragement to share. Just enough cash to buy their next high.

"Just think, when you have your own kid, you'll start your own fan club," Venus, the lead singer who lived in her VW van said. "You're gonna love that life."

Edgar was the only one in the group who hadn't slept with her. Before he married Georgina, I doubt he had the desire. "Yeah, my little rock star. Can't wait."

"When's it due, man?" Hairbone, the drummer, asked.

"I dunno. We have to figure that out. Gigi looks like a pumpkin though. Seems like it should be pretty soon."

Everyone laughed and nodded. In truth, he hadn't thought at all about the baby. That would be something for his parents and Georgina to deal with after he was gone.

The more time he spent with the band, the more he realized they were his "people". More than his brothers or Georgina or anyone he knew in high school. Venus knew that look; every time she belted out the high notes to the song he wrote, "Psychedelic Toe", he wanted to make her his.

One night, he waited until practice ended to approach Venus. "I was wondering if I could see your van?" he asked innocently.

Venus eyed him cautiously. "You sure about that? I just spread love where I can. You're the one who has strings attached."

"I'm sure." He winked.

That night, he went home with Venus's homemade perfume on him and scratch marks on his back. Surely he felt as though he was missing out, being stuck in Pepperville with a crying, misshapen girl and a dead-end job.

Georgina was pretending to be asleep, her hair splayed out across the pillow. "Gigi, you awake?"

"Huh?" She sat up and rubbed her eyes. "I must've fallen asleep waiting for you."

"We have to talk."

She looked over at the clock. "Right now? It's 11:30. Can't it wait?"

Edgar shook his head. "No, it's eating me up inside."

She took his hand and rubbed it with her own,

something she began recently. It irritated him for a reason he didn't understand.

"What is it, babe?"

"This thing... between us. It isn't working. I'll still pay for the kid, or I'm sure my dad will and whatever, but I don't want to live here anymore."

She dropped his hand. "Oh. I see. And what do you think I'm supposed to do? With your kid? Am I just going to be out on the street?"

"No, you can probably stay here. You know we have this place for a year. My parents wouldn't kick you out. At least my dad wouldn't... Maybe when the kid is old enough, you both can come join me in San Francisco." Edgar squirmed thinking about a baby interrupting his practice time.

"What? You're going without me?" Tears flowed down her face. Poor girl had nothing. No one.

"No, I—just at first. And then when I get settled, I'll come back for you. You and the kid can join me. It'll work out better this way. I just need some space to get myself off the ground with this music thing. You understand." He looked at the dresser, not daring to hold her gaze.

Georgina pulled back the covers and went to the closet. She took all her clothes and threw them on the floor.

"What are you doing? It's almost midnight!"

"You want me out, I'll leave."

Edgar grabbed her hand and pulled her back to the bed. "I don't want you out. It's me, I just need to get out before I go crazy. I'm not going to be a good dad if I'm unhappy. I'll find a great band and then I'll be in a place

96

for all the family stuff. For little Foghat." He began kissing her neck and pushed her back on the bed. For once, she didn't resist.

After work the next day, he came home and all of Georgina's things were packed into boxes and suitcases. She was sitting, with her coat on, waiting for him. He had been relieved to get the phone call over his lunch hour. His co-worker thought he might have cried a little when he thought no one was looking.

Gigi sat patiently while he made several trips up and down the stairs with boxes and finally came back for her suitcases. "Ready?" he asked.

"I'm ready," she said, smiling the fake smile that used to concern him. He noticed she was wearing lots of makeup and looked almost pretty.

They drove out into the country, over rolling green hills, and stopped when they arrived in front of a fancy, wrought-iron gate. Edgar didn't even try making conversation; it didn't seem necessary. Georgina was staring out the window with her hands resting on the lump that used to be her flat stomach. I hope he used that time for reflection. To feel guilt for his quick roll in the hay with Venus. Maybe for the way he treated the poor girl who had been turned away by everyone. Doubt it though.

A weather-beaten red truck pulled up behind them and someone in dirt-stained jeans got out and knocked on Georgina's window.

"You ready?" Kenneth, looking more muscular than when she saw him two months prior, peered in the window.

Georgina nodded. After Kenneth and Edgar had moved all her things from Edgar's Superbird to the back of the pickup, she got out.

Edgar stuck out his hand. "Thanks, man. Be cool. I'll see ya 'round."

"You don't have to thank me." My Kenneth shook Edgar's hand out of politeness. I taught him politeness above all. "I'd do anything for Gigi."

Edgar walked over to Georgina and tried to kiss her goodbye, but she turned her head. "Good luck in San Francisco," Georgina said curtly before getting into the passenger side of the truck.

Chapter 13

Georgina

"YOU'LL LOVE MY mom. She's been my best friend my whole life." Kenneth looked over at me and saw the tears soaking into the collar of my pink maternity blouse. "Don't worry about a thing, Gigi. This is all gonna work out."

The truck bounced to a stop in front of the imposing, two-story house. There were several rocking chairs on the grand porch that stretched around the entire front portion of the house. That space alone was larger than my parents' house. Even though it was still winter, macramé planters filled with a decorative green vine hung around the porch.

"I would be happy just living there," I remarked, wiping the grime of the ride from my forehead with the back of my hand. I reached down for the box of records sitting between my feet.

"Don't do that. I'll get those for you. We'll get you all settled and I can bring your stuff inside."

I smiled. "Thank you, Kenneth. Without you, I would have been living on the street. My folks don't want me back and I'm sure Edgar's parents would have kicked me out sooner or later."

When Edgar left for work, I called Kenneth immediately. He was out in the field, but his mother answered. "I need him. It's... complicated."

"You need a place to go, hon?" she asked. She seemed to understand without my saying much of anything. For once, I was grateful Kenneth shared everything with her.

I was in the grasp of a raging river, bobbing up and down as I headed toward the cliff. She reached her hand out and grabbed me.

"I wouldn't let the mother of my baby live on the street. Neither would my folks. They are tickled pink about the new grandbaby."

I blushed. He went around and opened the door and gently helped me to the ground. Kenneth continued to hold my hand as we went up the steps to the large porch, past the rockers, and through the wooden door with a lion's head knocker.

"Mom, we're here," he called.

A muscular, dark-haired woman with symmetrically cut short hair, bangs cut straight across her forehead, appeared from out of nowhere. She was wiping her glasses on her apron, and when she placed them on her face, I was shocked to see they looked like popular men's frames—thick, black plastic. She wasn't anything like the sweet grandmotherly-type I pictured from our phone call.

"Well, there's our girl!" She extended a hand and shook mine firmly. "I'm Frannie. Don't bother with the Mrs. Brownwell nonsense."

"Hello, Frannie. Pleased to meet you." I'd never been in a home so grand, and I wasn't sure how to act. Should I curtsey? I settled for a slight bow.

"Kenneth, Dad called on the radio. He's gonna need you over on the South forty. You bring in her things and I'll show her 'round the place."

"Yes'm." Kenneth smiled. "Sure is good having you here, Gigi."

He touched my back gently. I flinched, unused to a man's hand anywhere near me.

"Oh, is that what you like to be called? Seems like an odd nickname." Frannie motioned for me to follow her.

"You can call me whatever, Mrs.... I mean, Frannie."

I noticed several more macramé hangers containing leafy, cascading plants hanging around the main living room. There was a large painting over the mantle above the fireplace of a cowboy seated on a brown-and-white horse. The corners of his mouth were turned upward and he was touching his tall hat as if to invite city dwellers such as myself to join him on his journey.

As we headed up the grand staircase, I marveled at the fancy woodwork all around. It was like a museum. At the top of the landing was a life-sized portrait of a serious-looking woman. Her hair was swept up like the pictures of old Hollywood in my teen magazines. A fur stole wrapped around her shoulders and her hands were on her hips as if scolding whoever dared gaze at her.

"Is that your grandmother?" I whispered. It seemed like the right volume for a museum, where I felt I'd landed.

Kenneth, standing a few steps down with a box in his hands, guffawed. "Not hardly. My grandparents couldn't afford that kind of get up. That's the mother of the man who sold us the farm. For almost nothing. He just wanted to get out of here. He made us promise we would keep that thing hangin' up here forever. What's her name, Mom?"

"Millie. Horrible old shrew, by the looks of it."

I thought of all the rumors floating around about the farm. That it was haunted by some ghost hellbent on revenge. It was one of the excuses people used to steer clear of Kenneth.

"Let me show you to your room." Frannie directed me to the second door down a long hallway. The bed was so tall it was hard to sit on, even with my long legs. Everything was green. It reminded me of the mono-chromatic room where I caught my best friend and boyfriend together. It seemed so long ago.

"Now, if you're up for it, we'll take a little drive around the farm so you can get a feel for the place. I usually take the motorcycle, easy little thing to drive, but you're not in any condition for that." Frannie smiled and I could see her front two teeth were chipped.

"Thank you so much for taking me in."

Frannie sighed. "My Ken is just about the day and night for me. He tells me everything. The evening you two, well, did *this*," she made a circle in the air around my belly. "The night that happened, he came home and told me. He was excited. He's been in love with you since freshman year. This isn't the way I wanted things to happen for him, but we'll make the best of it. I've made an appointment with a doctor tomorrow for you. And you two should get married at some point. I don't tend to care what folks think, but you don't help your child any if the

parents aren't husband and wife." My chest tightened. I nodded.

"Okay, follow me." After we toured both floors, Frannie announced she would show me the newer version of Kenneth's truck in the main barn. On the way, we stopped at a large, barren patch of ground with colorful rocks piled at one end. "This doesn't look like anything now, but soon my garden will come to life. After family comes my garden. I grow prize-winning strawberries, for one. When the time comes, you can come out and help me if you want."

That sounded incredibly boring. I was hoping... well, maybe I fantasized in the short hours between life with Edgar and my transition to life with Kenneth that I would spend my days being waited on by servants, but so far I hadn't seen any. That was part of my motivation for calling Kenneth that morning, if I was being honest with myself. The Brownwells, while living in a grander home, lived more humbly than Edgar's family.

"There's a nice chicken coop on the other side of the barn. I didn't want anything more to do with poultry after we share-cropped. Some days I still think I smell like a chicken." Frannie laughed—a loud, deep laugh. "I said, 'Hon, you want 'em, you feed 'em.' And that's just what he did. Named each of the seven hens after the days of the week. So, Harlan could come in and tell us he has Friday eggs when it's Tuesday."

I smiled and nodded. There was no humor in my home, so it felt strange to think Kenneth's parents joked about things.

We got into the bright red pickup and drove around the perimeter of the farm—ten square miles. Frannie showed me where they planted the winter wheat, where the corn would go, and all the buildings for grain storage. We stopped on top of a hill. "You okay getting out?"

I nodded. My feet ached, but I was embarrassed to tell Frannie, a woman who didn't seem to have an off button. I surveyed the land around us—rolling hills for miles, just as Kenneth had described. There was no sound except for the slight breeze that whistled around me.

"We call it Spud Hill. You can see all four corners of our place from here. I like to come up here to think sometimes. Can't believe that I own all of this. I started my marriage with one pair of pants to my name. It's hard to believe."

A *swoosh* of air blew up my pants and startled me. "Awwk!" I jumped backward, noticing to my surprise that there was a vent in the ground.

"Oh, sorry, hon. That's for the potato cellar. We're standing on an artificial hill. Underneath is a big space where we used to store the potatoes we grew. And after that," Frannie put her hand beside her mouth as if she needed to whisper on this lonely spot, "somebody built themselves a still. Potato vodka. We don't like folks to know about that, so keep it under your hat."

I giggled. "Don't worry, I don't have anyone to tell." I was sorry I shared that. I didn't want Frannie thinking I was an outcast. Like her son.

Frannie put her hands on her hips. "We sure are happy to have you here. Harlan and I tried forever to have children before Ken. Never could make things work. So now our boy is our world. Like I told you this morning, you matter to him, so you matter to us."

"I... don't know how to be a mother," I blurted. I thought about all the hours I spent with my younger brothers, only half-interested in what they said or did, just like my parents. The children in my house weren't anyone's world.

"No one does, hon. But I'll be here to help you every step of the way." Frannie smiled. "We'll do just fine. You make your child the center of everything and you've really left your mark."

We got back into the pickup and drove down the hill to the large opening where the potatoes were stored. "Do you want to see the still? It's got historical value, I suppose."

The last thing I wanted to do was get out of the car again. My entire body ached. Maybe it had every day before, but I had been so miserable I hadn't paid attention. "That would be great."

Frannie drove into the dark tunnel and switched the pickup lights to bright. "See that little room up to the right? That's where the still is. Looks like they were bottling things up and had to leave in a hurry. I don't know why anyone hasn't come out here and taken care of it."

"I'm feeling a little tired. Would it be okay if we went back home?" *Was it home?* Nothing felt like home.

"Of course, hon. Off we go."

When we returned to the big house, a wonderful smell of something that must be a real dinner surrounded us. My stomach rumbled.

"Can you set the table, Gigi?"

Never once in my previous life did I set a table. There were no delicately flowered plates placed on the table in anticipation of dinner at the Hardwick home. I wasn't even sure where the silverware should go. "I'm... we didn't do this often at my house. Maybe you could show me, just this once."

"What am I thinking? Poor girl. You're probably exhausted. Maybe you just sit while I do it tonight."

I smiled and let out a sigh of relief. "Okay!"

After Frannie set the last glass on the long, formal table, the kitchen door opened. "Shoes, boys!" she commanded.

I was trying to memorize the placement of each item on the table, but exhaustion controlled my every thought.

The scent of sweat mixed with dirt drifted into the dining area. As I concentrated on keeping my eyelids in the upright position, Kenneth entered the room carrying steaming dishes of corn and mashed potatoes. He winked at me.

"My dad's coming. He's been excited to meet you all day."

I resisted the urge to roll my eyes. Only Kenneth would think an old man would be excited to meet a pregnant teenager.

Harlan Brownwell, a tall man with bushy brown eyebrows, a big nose, and full wide lips, sat down directly across from me.

"'Lo, there. Harlan Brownwell. I'm Kenneth's dad." He didn't look directly at me. He absently pushed the few remnants of grey hair to one side of his head before offering his hand across the table. I strained across my belly to reach it.

"I'm Georgina Pep... um... Hardwick." I smiled my fake smile.

Frannie made several trips, carrying a gravy boat, a platter of roast beef, rolls, and mixed vegetables to the table. It was more food than I had ever seen in one place.

"Your father owns the shoe store?" Harlan asked.

I couldn't stop shoveling food in, so I answered with a full mouth. "No, he's the manager." I couldn't muster shame for the bits of potato catapulting to the white tablecloth.

"Well, it's a darn shame he don't want to know his grandbaby. He don't know what he's missin'."

My heart swelled. "Thank you, sir."

"Now don't be callin' me that. I'm Harlan. Never been a sir."

"Dad, tell her about the ghost," Kenneth insisted. "He's full of secrets. Says he's gonna put a whole section in his will so we'll have to listen for once." He winked at me for the second time.

"No real story 'bout any ghosts. Sometimes when Kenneth was little, he'd be afraid of someone comin' to cart him off so we would pretend to scare the ghosts away from his room. That's because we used to have a farm hand who told him stories of a boogeyman who hid between the milk cows. One time he popped out and scared ole Ken when we was fixin' to milk and darned if I couldn't get that boy back out to the barn for almost a year."

I chuckled politely. I remembered how many people teased him for being different. I laughed at him several times behind his back. Maybe we were afraid of ghosts too.

"That and Aunt Katherine always telling me I was lucky to live here. She seemed to think I had any choice in the matter. It was the way she said it, bending over real close to my face like it was a dark secret. Always made me look over my shoulder for the boogey-man," Kenneth added, scooping another helping of meat onto his plate. "Not worried about that anymore though."

Frannie and Harlan exchanged a glance. "That farm hand works at Lecher Farm now. Got a speeding ticket last month. You watch out for him when you're on the road, Ken."

Harlan pushed his plate toward the middle of the table and sat back in the chair. "There's lots of history in this old place. Did you know that back at the turn of the century, there was a poor house where this place is today? Big old building for folks to live who didn't have anything of their own. Those folks worked the farm, ate what they grew, and lived a simple life."

I mulled over my current situation. How, if I had lived then, I would have been living in just that manner. Something that hadn't seemed possible just a few months earlier.

Frannie spooned more vegetables on my plate and then took the roll from her own and gave it to me. "You're looking a little underweight. When we get you in to the doctor, we'll make sure he feels you're doing okay. We can't have our grandchild born ill."

I started to protest, but I was hungrier than I realized. It had been so long since I'd had a real meal.

"I took her out to show her the property today. That potato cellar has to go. I've been telling you boys that for years now."

"Yes'm." Kenneth was shoveling roast into his mouth at a rate similar to mine.

"You always tell me that, but nothing ever happens. I don't want my grandchildren getting hurt."

Either you boys take care of it, or I just might go out there one of these days and do it myself." Harlan chuckled. "I have no doubt about that. Don't you worry, we'll take care of it."

Frannie insisted that I rest in the formal living room after dinner instead of helping with dishes. "We don't waste food here, so expect to see leftovers for a few days," she called.

"Oh, I don't mind," I put my feet up on the coffee table, embarrassed by their swollen state. I hoped no one walked in while I was propped up. "We never ate that fancy at my house. I'd eat that for days."

"I'm excited to find out when you're due," Frannie called, clattering dishes in the sink. "I have a good idea, but the doctor will know for sure."

Her chatter dimmed in my head until there was just sweet silence. I couldn't keep my eyes open any longer.

Chapter 14

Georgina

"MRS. BROWNWELL, I know you find it important to come in with the girl, but I'm going to have to insist you stay outside until I'm done with the examination." Doctor Andrews adjusted his glasses as he stood, blocking the doorway of the treatment room.

"It's my grandchild though, Harry. I need to know what to expect. We've got to prepare the house for the little one." Frannie stood inches from him, hands on her hips. "I'm paying for the appointment. I do insist."

Dr. Andrews shook his head. "You know how much I admire you, Francine. Especially after you helped with the Jackson quintuplets, doing all the laundry and cleaning for that family for months. But on this, I'm going to remain firm. If you would like to wait in the waiting room, Georgina can update you when we're finished. I'm sure she'll give you all the pertinent details of our conversation."

Frannie huffed and then peeked past his folded arms to the examination table, where I sat uncomfortably, arms folded over my paper gown. "I'll expect a full update then. Perhaps you can write me up a report, so I can share it with Harlan and Kenneth."

"Maybe." Doctor Andrews stepped inside and pulled the door closed behind him. He smiled at me. "Now then. I'm sorry about that. Frannie can be a bit assertive. The poor woman experienced an uncertain childhood and now seems to try and control everything around her. She tells me things about my office I'd never know otherwise." He chuckled. "Don't know if she digs through the trash at night or what her secret is. But, that being said, I've never known anyone more fiercely protective of their family. Frannie's a good woman. No one better to have on your side."

I nodded. After I had to remove the enormous striped smock dress (that had been laying on my bed this morning) under Frannie's watchful eye, I was more than relieved we wouldn't be sharing the examination room space. Frannie insisted on touching my belly while I was standing completely naked. She told me it was "only normal".

"Can you give me the date of your last cycle?"

I blushed. I didn't want to talk about this with a strange man. "I don't know. I didn't really keep track. Sometime in the fall."

"I see. Let me measure you and we'll see what we come up with." He placed the tape measure over my large abdomen. "Frannie says her boy is quite smitten with you. Lucky girl."

I thought about my many trysts with Edgar. How I would dream about touching him when we weren't together. Even when his words bored me, it was the one thing we always had in common. I couldn't even remember that one night with Kenneth, just that he was wearing the same cologne Edgar wore.

Someday, Kenneth might question if the baby is his, and I would be out on the street once more. As kind as his parents were, they wouldn't want a girl and a stranger's baby living under their roof. All of this was making my stomach hurt. I hoped there was no way for the doctor to figure out I'd been with two men. I had no idea how these things worked.

"My estimate is early summer. We'll get you on a hearty diet so that your weight increases as it should.

My nurse will discuss things further."

"And... that's all... you need to know?" I stuttered.

Dr. Andrews smiled and patted my knee. "Don't worry. I've delivered hundreds of babies. They always make an entrance when they're ready. You'll be just fine. Francine will make sure of that."

Frannie jumped out of her chair when I appeared in the waiting room. "What did he say? When is our little wonder coming?"

"In a month or two. He thinks my iron may be a bit low. He suggested drinking dark beer." I scrunched my nose. "I don't like beer." I hoped it was convincing enough for Kenneth's mother.

Frannie ushered me out the office door. "We're not doing that. I'm not convinced one should drink or smoke while pregnant. Doesn't seem natural. We'll keep you well fed though." As we drove down Main Street, Frannie pulled up a few spaces away from the Shoppe and Walke. She turned and put her hand on my knee. "I know this is too hard for you. I've got to get a few more groceries. Those farmhands have a hole somewhere. The more I make, the more they eat. You can wait in the car."

"Thank you, Mrs.... Frannie."

I sat and watched as my future mother-in-law walked confidently into the store where my mother worked for most of my life. There were times I looked forward to stopping in after school to say hi to her. There was always a caramel waiting for me next to the cash register.

We would talk about everything I learned in school that day. "You're going to grow up to be the smartest girl in the class, Georgina. Someday you'll do great things." I felt good, knowing my mother appreciated me.

When the twins were born, she just seemed tired and irritated all the time. There were no more caramels at the checkout. Just a vacant woman who was going through the motions of her day. "Better get home and get your chores done," she would say when I tried to surprise her, hoping for a happy reception.

Eventually, I stopped visiting her. I couldn't bear to be brushed aside. In order to ease my mother's burden, I began bathing the boys at night and putting them to bed. By the time I was in the seventh grade, Mildred and Bob realized there was no longer a need to spend money on daycare for the boys when I was perfectly capable of doing it for them.

For just a moment, I considered going into the store. If I hugged my mother somewhere so public, she wouldn't be able to run away. But I knew that would end badly. Mildred didn't take kindly to being ambushed.

The wind picked up and caught the door as Frannie opened it. She held on tightly, her bicep muscles bulging in her tight, stretch-knit top. "I saw your mother briefly. I told her you were living with us now. She seemed rather shocked."

I tugged at the sailor collar on my dress. "Did Kenneth tell you where I was living before?"

Frannie backed out and we continued our journey through town. "Of course, he did. He tells me everything, remember?"

"Did he tell you I'm married to Edgar? I had no choice..."

"I know EVERYTHING, hon." Frannie smiled— a wide, knowing smile that would have looked unsettling on anyone else. "As soon as Kenneth told me you were marrying another boy, even though you had his baby in your belly, I went to the courthouse. Well, I stop once a week to pick up the police report and any other public records, so it wasn't like I made an extra trip. You'll be relieved to know you're not really married to that creepy kid." She shook her head, forcing every straight piece of shiny hair back into its symmetrical place. We watched as a giant tumbleweed blew across the road in front of us.

"I don't understand."

"Edgar's cousin, Marybeth, is not well-liked at the courthouse. Apparently, not very bright either. She signed as your guardian on the application, but on the actual license, she signed her own name instead of your mother's. Once I pointed that out, her boss was only too happy to call her in and give her the once-over. She's no longer employed there."

I felt guilty for getting Edgar's cousin involved. I wondered if Edgar knew. There was a lightness knowing I was no longer attached to anyone else's life.

"You and Ken can get married at any time. I was thinking next week. I have a dress I can alter. You can get married in the courtyard. I haven't shown you that area yet, but we've planted lots of bushes and a couple of nice trees. Harlan even made a bench."

The very last thing I wanted to do was get married again. "I'm not sure. Shouldn't we wait?"

"And have my grandbaby considered a bastard? I mostly don't care what folks think of me, but that's where I draw the dad-gum line. No sirree; we're doing things legal this time. I'll bring the form to your mom, I'm sure she'll sign if I ask in front of her boss. And I've got a great recipe for wedding cake."

It was shocking to think about how much planning Frannie already put into an event I hadn't agreed to yet. I imagined myself moving into Kenneth's room as strangers. Our night together was spontaneous, and I didn't remember much of it. He was a friend, but the thought of his touch when I was sober was too much. I would have to lay next to him every night. As his wife. I started feeling nauseous. "Can you pull over?"

Before the truck rolled to a stop, I reached my head out the door and vomited. Frannie came around to the passenger side with a rag and began wiping my face. "It's normal to have those waves of ick clear up 'til the end, hon. Don't worry about it."

We sat in silence for several minutes until my stomach calmed. I looked out over the field of broken corn stalks and saw cattle behind a barbed wire fence, staring at the round woman vomiting in their field. They had no choices in their lives either.

"Can we do the wedding next week?"

Frannie did her best to pull everything together. My feet ached as I stood, while Frannie endlessly poked me with pins.

"Sorry, hon!" Frannie stayed up until almost dawn several nights, sewing feverishly. When I finally saw myself in the mirror, I was at once horrified and pleased.

"I look like a snowball!" I cried. On someone else, it would have been lovely. The empire-waisted dress with floppy sleeves displayed a slight bit of beading, waving its way across my increasingly large bust. The skirt was long and wide enough to accommodate Frannie's impending grandbaby. It might have been two dresses sewn together, for all the material hanging on me.

"No, hon, you look like a beautiful bride. I got you a

floppy hat to match, but you've got such beautiful hair, maybe we should just curl it up and put some flowers in."

I shrugged. I'd given up trying to have an opinion. I just didn't care. It seemed like Frannie was right about most things anyway.

The wedding took place in the courtyard area behind the house. Frannie was right—it was beautiful. The purple, white, and pink trumpet-shaped clusters of phlox just started blooming and their intoxicating scent filled the space. Frannie rented a tent and even agreed to pay two farmhands to hold it steady in case of wind. In addition to a three-tiered lavender cake, she spent days making mints, candies, and cookies.

There was no one I could think of to invite. In another lifetime, Lois would have been my maid of honor. We would have giggled over her bridesmaid dress. She would pick something completely unflattering and I would find just the right style for her round body. Round like mine. We weren't so different anymore.

When Frannie went into the grocery store to get the marriage application signed, I asked her to invite Mildred. As expected, she politely declined. "Quite stuck on the fact that it's your second marriage," Frannie commented. Other than Lois and Edgar, there was no one I'd spent time with the last two years of high school. In attendance were three neighbor couples, a judge who was a friend of Harlan's, and Harlan's sister, Katherine.

Katherine planned to be in Pepperville for Kenneth's high school graduation. She came from just over the Iowa border, the Illinois town of Moline to be exact. Since graduation was the day after the wedding, she agreed to arrive a day early. A tall woman with a long face, dark eyes, and dark, bushy brows, she was an intimidating presence.

"Katherine Brownwell. Pleased to meet you, miss." She shook my hand so firmly it knocked me off balance. Katherine grabbed me with both arms and righted me.

"Young lady, you need to get some exercise so that body of yours doesn't become infirmed." Katherine patted me soundly on the back. "I'm surprised farm life hasn't made a strong woman of you already." She pushed up her round, wire-rimmed glasses and shook her head. "Not one for children. In fact, I have an intense dislike. Rarely seen and even more rarely heard. That's my motto."

"Katherine was a schoolteacher. She was always excellent with Kenneth, don't let her fool you, Gigi." Frannie smiled as she passed by carrying a tray of punch cups.

"I strongly disagree with Francine. I was only part of Kenneth's life after he developed a sense of reason and an understanding of his place in the world. I'll be pleased if you understand that's my level of interest in Kenneth's offspring as well."

I smiled weakly. I still hadn't learned how to interact comfortably with Kenneth's family. They spoke in their own language, inside jokes and farm words that sounded foreign. "You'll understand soon, Gigi," Kenneth remarked almost every night, patting my leg.

"What do you do, Miss Brownwell?"

"What do you mean, 'do?' I'm an old, retired woman. My 'do' consists of charity work and avoiding people who refer to me as 'Miss Brownwell'."

I blushed. It was becoming my natural color.

"I'm sorry..."

"*Ma'am* will do."

I walked down the makeshift aisle, a cobblestone pathway, holding onto Harlan's arm. Kenneth was shaking, tears pouring down his face. Frannie had mentioned a big surprise for Kenneth, and it was apparent now they purchased a two-tone brown plaid suit for the occasion. His hair was combed to the side and smoothed with a styling aid that made him look like someone from the old gangster movies I used to watch after the boys went to bed.

I took his arm and also noticed, to my delight, that he was wearing Edgar's favorite cologne, *Manly*. He did look handsome, in a less obvious way than Edgar. His clear blue eyes shone in the sunlight and his smile was warm and loving. Another girl might have even found him attractive.

"You look like an angel," he whispered.

When the judge was done and pronounced us man and wife, Kenneth leaned in to kiss me. I hadn't kissed anyone since my last night with Edgar. I knew it was coming, yet my first instinct was to pull away. Especially in front of his parents. I was surprised that it wasn't as unpleasant as I thought it might be. I could feel his desire and wished for a moment that I shared those feelings. He deserved that.

"Love you, Mrs. Brownwell!" he said softly. I smiled.

I started feeling sick after eating my second piece of cake. Frannie insisted we not waste any scrap of food and, consequently, we often ate leftovers until well past what I deemed safe. Sometimes the meat developed a blue tint, which Frannie cut off the edge and served. I was sure this must be the cause of my unsettled stomach.

I found Kenneth, who was having a serious discussion about crop yields with the judge, and tugged on his sleeve. "I'm going to lie down. I don't feel great."

"Okay, dear. In your old room or new?" He winked.

I blushed. He said the most awkward things. "Maybe tomorrow night." I didn't know how long I would be able to keep him away. Something that felt so natural with Edgar was now the very thing I dreaded the most.

I went to bed thankful for my discomfort. It kept me from thinking about what I'd just done, how I'd committed myself to a life with someone I barely knew out of desperation.

The following morning, the day of Kenneth's graduation, I woke up feeling worse. I hobbled down to the kitchen, where Frannie was scrambling eggs with chopped up bits of two-nights-ago hot dogs mixed in.

"I don't feel well. Do you have something that might help?"

Frannie wiped her hands on her apron and felt my forehead. "Don't feel feverish." She put her hands on my belly, something that was growing tiresome.

For once, I pushed my new mother-in-law's fingers away. "No, I don't want you to touch me. I feel awful." A puddle of fluid splashed onto the tiled kitchen floor around my feet.

"We won't be going to graduation today, hon. We need to get you to the hospital."

Chapter 15

Frannie

FRANCINE DELBA-MARIE BAILEY (my name from birth) and my older-yet-identical sister, Marga-rine Beatrice Bailey, slept in the same bed in the living room of our parents' one-bedroom, mud-colored home. Margarine always slept with one protective arm around me. We were afraid of what might come in the night, thanks to Papa's story-telling.

Every tale included a blood-thirsty, wealthy villain ready to snatch little princesses, always named Margarine and Francine, from their beds and take them to his evil mansion lair for dissection. When Delbert Fredrick Bailey became too descriptive in his tale of one villain or another, Margarine would put her hands over my ears. "Continue with caution, Papa."

My daddy Delbert worked as a farmhand when he wasn't driving a truck. He often changed his mind about what he wanted to do with his life but never wavered in his desire to write stories about monsters and princesses. When we couldn't afford notebooks, he scribbled his stories on the day-old newspapers he found in the trashcans around town. Since he wrote in the white space around the page, it was often difficult to know which way to turn the paper to read the next section. It didn't matter. His fantasy world both fascinated and horrified his girls. His main character, at least in the stories he told us, was a plucky princess named Eugenia who got herself out of seemingly impossible situations each time.

Jelica Bailey, Mama, did her best to keep a routine no matter what her husband's latest whim, work or otherwise. She always promised us that someday we would be able to purchase fine clothing and eat steaks and pork chops like other people in Pepperville.

When Margarine and I were in high school, Papa became ill. He didn't want to spend his precious few dollars on a doctor so, instead, I quit school to work at the mill and provide the family with an extra income. In my off hours, I did clothing repairs and hemming.

He died the October of what would have been my senior year. The doctor at the hospital told my papa, who only sought treatment when he could no longer write his stories, he would have survived his disease if he had been treated earlier. Papa was always adamant he didn't want to waste our grocery money.

Since I'd already quit school, I went to work at Lecher Farm, helping to care for chickens, clean coops, and tend their massive garden. I didn't mind it so much. The Lechers were not the evil people of my papa's scary tales, they just expected hard work from those in their employ. And then there was the biggest perk—Harlan

Brownwell, a lanky, dark-haired farmhand who always smiled and tipped his hat when we crossed paths.

Stolen moments together in the main barn led to handholding behind the chicken coops. Whenever Harlan found a free moment, he found me and pretended he needed my help with something. I looked forward to his gentle kisses. The other farmhands joked that the Lecher Farms Romance would find its way into the *Pepperville Daily Times*, not in the Society section but under Farm and Ranch Happenings.

When we decided to marry, Harlan was eager to start our own family. After three miscarriages, I told Harlan it was probably for the best that we didn't have children. We were just as poor as my parents had been and children, from my childhood memories, were always something of a burden. I resigned myself to the idea of motherhood not being a part of my life.

When I became pregnant again three years later, I was wary. As my pregnancy progressed and my belly grew to the size of my pregnant friends', I allowed myself to become excited. All the farmhands threw me a baby shower when it became apparent the pregnancy would succeed.

The day came to go to the hospital. The doctor told Harlan he could leave the hospital for a bit, but he insisted on staying by his wife's side as long as possible. As I was wheeled away to give birth to our first child, he kissed my cheek. "Can't say as I've ever been so darned proud of anyone, Frannie. Gonna finally make me a daddy." I smiled, thinking of the baby clothes my sister made and the hours I would spend on the tiny porch, rocking my sweet child, a clone of Harlan.

When I awoke from the anesthesia, the doctor and a nurse were standing beside my bed with somber faces. "Your daughter did not survive the womb. We never know the reasons for these things." The doctor refused to look me in the eye. Not uncommon for the day but hurtful nonetheless.

"I see no reason why you can't have more children." He turned abruptly and left the room.

The nurse came to my side and held my hand. "I went through the same thing last year. I'm so sorry."

It didn't seem possible that life could hate me this much. "Can I see my baby?" I asked through my tears. "I want to hold my daughter."

"Oh no, we don't do that. You're better off not seeing the child. It will only make your grief harder."

"I want to see my baby. It's MY baby. Just once— please!" I squeezed her arm, not allowing her to move away.

The nurse nodded and I loosened my grip so she could leave the room. She returned a short time later with a thick swaddle of pink blanket. "Just for a minute. I could lose my job for this. I'll stand at the door and watch."

I opened the blanket and saw a perfectly formed child. Her perfect nose was long, just like Harlan's. Her tiny head displayed a shock of dark hair. She would have been the perfect addition to our little family. I kissed her head and held her tiny body to my chest. "Eugenia Brownwell. You have my heart."

When the nurse took her away, I resolved never to go through the pain of losing a child again. The focus of my life, when I wasn't working on the section of Lecher

Farm we were sharecropping, was my husband. I didn't need friendships or any kind of relationships outside of the ones with Harlan and his sister Katherine. My life was crumbling away.

Harlan came home one day with news neither of us anticipated. "I bought a farm."

"What? Harlan, how can that be? We can barely feed the two of us." I was sewing a new sequined dress for Mrs. Ashton, a rich lady who lived in town. What the wealthy would do with such finery in Pepperville was beyond me.

"He was desperate to leave town. Sold it to me for $100. He's going to help finance. I know it sounds like the craziest darn thing, but this is our chance to live a better life, Frannie. You'll have to trust me. Things is going to be better from now on for all of us."

When you have years of bad, you don't trust that good things know the way to your doorstep. Being given a chance at our own farm seemed like our one and only dose, and we were grateful. But somehow our luck continued.

Kenneth Harlan Brownwell's unexpected arrival came at just the right time, before I was irretrievably lost to my grief. I found the boxes of clothes a neighbor helpfully packed away labeled "Smaller Fabric Items." The sounds of an infant brought new life to me, and in turn to Harlan. We strapped him to our backs to perform chores. As he got older, he chased chickens around the yard while I cleaned the coops and recovered eggs.

Living on the big farm was perfect for Kenneth. He thrived in such a grand space, learning from his father during the day and becoming a good student in the evenings under the supplemental tutelage of his mother.

Though I didn't have friends, I did try my best to keep Margarine and my mother in my life. Margarine, after being subjected to years of my father's scary stories about wealthy people, was wary of her sister's new world. Rumors, mostly false, about the farm and how the Brownwells acquired it swirled into every nook and cranny of Pepperville. Eventually, Margarine and my mama cut off all communication with us.

I cornered Margarine one day when I was at the Shoppe and Walke. I grabbed her arm tightly. "Why won't you look at me?"

She stared at the ground with eyes the mirror of mine. "You know. You and your husband. I hear things." She slithered from my grasp and ran outside.

I didn't know. I had no idea, until I started asking around, that the entire community decided Harlan and I, former-sharecropping simple people suddenly possessed some otherworldly powers, or the kindship of a helpful ghost that caused us to acquire this farm. It was silly and unsettling. This circle of misinformation was happening without my knowledge. I felt completely helpless and set about making sure I was never surprised by rumors again.

I had to protect myself and my family. First, I planted a large garden, similar to the one I tended on Lecher Farm. I loved the quiet and the space to think. Spinach, radishes, lettuce, peppers, onions, beans, and potatoes. I especially loved planting every type of strawberry I could get my hands on. I loved experimenting with berries, a delicate plant that required much love and care, to see how they would grow in this new soil. Brownwell soil. I nurtured them and watched them thrive. It finished sewing up the hole in my heart Eugenia left.

Second, I canned everything I grew, in anticipation of the day when my good fortune disappeared and the three of us were once more sharecropping. We wouldn't have to rely on anyone. I found a storm shelter not far from the barn where I could store everything I made. When that became too small, I planned a small addition to our home. I had built and repaired chicken coops at Lecher Farm and, with Harlan's help, I was able to build a simple room with plenty of shelving and a single lightbulb to store all my canned goods. We procured enough to weather any storm for years to come.

And third, I made sure that every dark corner of the town was exposed to daylight. There was nothing happening in this community, no matter how minute or unseemly, that didn't reach my ears. I would never be caught unaware again.

The day I showed my soon-to-be daughter-in-law around the farm, we only paused briefly at the garden. "This is my pride and joy." I motioned toward the newly-spaded soil where this year's seeds would grow. "Over there, at the far end, is my strawberry patch. I have four varieties right now. I've been growing a test batch for a few years—P90834. I think if they turn out, they'll name them after me.

I've already been calling them Franniebells."

Georgina nodded. I noticed she wasn't much for

conversation, not like the bubbly girl Kenneth had described so enthusiastically.

"Maybe you'll feel like helping me out in the garden, once the baby comes."

"Maybe." Georgina stared off at the barn across the yard. "I don't know anything about gardens though." Her maternity dress was blowing in the wind and she refused to push it back down. I thought she might be trying to test my patience.

"I think you're going to have a girl. That's my guess, anyhow. Would you consider naming her Eugenia? It's a name I've always favored."

Georgina pushed the hair out of her eyes. "I don't know. I guess. I haven't really given it any thought." Another gust of wind came up and her dress almost blew over her head.

"Let's go back inside. This weather doesn't work with maternity wear." I tried not to show my irritation. This girl cared about nothing. I also offered to let her go through Kenneth's baby things, but she refused.

The morning of Kenneth's graduation, I realized we may not be able to watch both our only child graduate and our first grandchild being born. "Katherine, would you want to stay at the hospital so we could watch Kenneth's graduation?" I asked as we were preparing the Impala for its most important trip to town.

Kenneth put his hand on Georgina's arm. "I'm not going, Mom! I have to be at the hospital for Georgina!"

"Son, these things take time. You'll most likely be able to graduate and be back before the baby comes.

There's nothing you can do besides sit in the waiting room."

I covered the seat and floor with towels. I'd seen enough farm births to know things got messy. "Careful, Gigi. Ease in slowly."

Georgina let out a howl. "It hurts. It really hurts."

"I'm not going to graduation. They can mail me the diploma. I have to be with my wife. That's my final decision." Kenneth slid in beside Georgina and took her hand. I stared at them for a moment, assessing what to do next. I felt a surge of pride watching my boy already protecting his family.

"I'm not going to attend any birth. You are well aware of my dislike of children before the age of ten. I'll happily smile through the graduation, as was my intended purpose for this trip." Katherine was standing behind me wearing her rose-colored Sunday dress and sensible black shoes. She was even wearing lipstick, a rare event.

"The boy don't want to go to graduation, dear. I'd much rather celebrate a beginnin' than an end myself. Let's go to the hospital," Harlan urged, ignoring his sister's comments.

There was no point in arguing with any of them. "Alright," I raised my hands in defeat, "we'll all go to the hospital. Get in, Harlan. Katherine, enjoy your time of peace at the farm."

Harlan got in the driver's seat, beside Georgina, who was doubled over in pain. Kenneth held a protective arm around her swollen body. I sat quietly in the back as we sped down the dirt road. I turned to see Katherine watching us long as she could, no doubt looking forward to a glass of lemonade and my copy of *The Many Loves of a Girl Named Lorla Lavendish* on the porch.

We sat in the waiting room for two-and-a-half hours. Kenneth paced back and forth, back and forth, before I sent him outside. "We'll come to get you when something happens. You need to go for a walk before you burn a hole in the floor."

Kenneth nodded obediently. After jogging twice around the building, peering through the window at us on each pass, he returned, shocked to see the doctor speaking to us. "Congratulations. You have a fine grandson. A bit early, but very healthy. You can go see him in the nursery if you would like."

Kenneth, out of breath and covered in sweat, ran to grab the doctor. "How's my Georgina? Is she okay?"

He smiled. "The girl is just fine. You can go see her now if you wish. She should be coming out of the anesthesia."

Kenneth nudged the doctor aside and ran through the hall, looking in each room until he found his wife. Harlan and I stopped at the nursery window. I pushed away the sadness that welled up. Memories of my Eugenia were hard to dismiss, even after all these years.

"He looks just like my dad. Same nose. Gonna be a handsome feller." Harlan sniffed a little, his way of pretending he wasn't crying.

I took Harlan's hand. It was rough and worn, especially so for a man of his age. It made me love him more, thinking of how hard he worked to make the farm a source of good income and a home for all of us. "It will be nice having another baby in the house. This time, we won't have to wash him with rainwater. He'll have the best."

We walked hand-in-hand to Georgina's room, where Kenneth was holding Georgina's hand, watching her adoringly as she stared in the opposite direction.

"He's a beautiful boy. What are we going to call him?" I went over and pulled the curtains open farther, displaying an overcast sky and a quiet Main Street.

"I don't care. You can name him." Georgina turned her head toward the window.

I suppressed my anger. This girl did everything she could to be disagreeable.

"Did you see your son, Kenneth? He's a beaut." Harlan squeezed his son's shoulder.

"Not yet, Dad. I'm waiting to walk down with Gigi when she feels like it."

"What if we named him after your dad? We could call him Harlan? Ryan Brownwell is also a fine name. After Grandpa Brownwell? Maybe Ryan Harlan, or Ryan Kenneth." I pulled a chair up to the bedside and patted Georgina's leg. "That sounds right, don't you think?"

Tears came to Harlan's eyes for the second time. "That's just about the nicest thing. But you know, I don't b'lieve we should make the boy feel like he has to match expectations of a life already lived. He needs to be his own man, built from scratch."

"Oh Harlan, that's nonsense. Kenneth has your middle name. But if you're feeling shy all of a sudden, we could use Grandpa and Kenneth's names together? We'd call him Kyan. Ryan and Kenneth mixed." I looked at my husband and smiled. "So, he can be his own man from scratch."

"I like that, Mom. Kyan Brownwell sounds like someone successful. What do you think, Gigi?"

Georgina folded her arms across her chest and stared as if there was something peculiar on the wall behind her new family. "Name him whatever you want. I don't care."

Chapter 16

Katherine

"DO YOU WANT me to feed him again?"
Francine stood in the doorway of Georgina's room, Kyan whimpering in her arms. Georgina nodded. I tried not to get involved, even if my curiosity over the unfolding situation kept me constantly hungry to observe.

"You'll have to get out of bed at some point," she commented halfheartedly. Francine didn't want Georgina's input on caring for her grandson. Kyan was the perfect baby, even more agreeable than Kenneth. I could tell she loved their time together in the middle of the night, rocking in the big chair as she stared out the picture window. Georgina may have given birth to him, but Kyan was hers.

"We'll go into town tomorrow. I may take him to the park in that new stroller. Maybe give you some time to yourself." I stifled a giggle. Georgina knew only of a life with time to herself, at least on this farm. She still hadn't moved into Kenneth's room and she spent her days in bed, often with the drapes closed.

When the tiny, high-pitched cries drifted into Harlan and Francine's bedroom for the second night in a row, Harlan rolled over and poked her in the ribs. "You hear that?"

I chuckled at the idea. "Francine, the poor man has hearing loss. He probably thought it was a sick dog in the yard."

"I told Harlan, 'Of course, I do. I haven't slept a wink. I'm going to go in and feed him. She probably doesn't know how, even though I showed her. They said she only visited the nursery twice the whole four days she was in the hospital.'"

"I got out of bed and Harlan told me to put on my slippers, you know, those fuzzy, blue ones he got me?" Francine continued. "Anyway, I went downstairs and fed the baby. Eventually, the crying stopped and I could hear Harlan snoring. On the third night, I brought the bassinet into our bedroom." Francine took a sip of coffee, jiggling the baby on her shoulder. "He only grumbled about it one time. 'I have to get up early,' he says. 'We're close to harvest. Can't you move that somewhere else?' Well, of course I could move him, but if he went, so did I. That was the last of it."

Kenneth eagerly awaited his turn feeding his newborn son as well. He came in on his lunch break, changed his grimy clothes, and washed his hands before placing the crocheted blanket over his lap in anticipation of his son's squirmy body.

He tried knocking on Georgina's door a few times at the end of the day, but she never answered.

Frannie tried comforting him. "Don't fret, son. She'll come around." I wasn't so sure she would. I'd never seen a mother so unattached to a child. After a frank discussion with my sister-in-law, I agreed to stay on at Brownwell Farm. It was clear circumstances called for an extra pair of hands, and my charity and aging could wait.

One day, I decided enough was enough. Francine agreed reluctantly. We had a system in place, and it didn't involve Georgina. Francine stood in the hallway as I turned the knob and marched in. I breathed in the stale smell of a room and a life shut off from the world. Not like the room of someone on the cusp of adulthood.

"It's time for you to start being energetic, Georgina. You live on a working farm and one of this size requires all hands be productive." I pulled the curtains open, releasing a cloud of dust.

Georgina shrugged. "I don't know how to do anything."

I put my hands on my generous hips. "Well, why didn't you say so earlier? I will gladly teach you. Poor Francine has that baby on one hip and a bushel of vegetables on the other. It's time you learned to garden."

I stared at Georgina until the girl reluctantly pulled the covers back. I yanked a maternity dress from a hanger in the closet. "These will need altering. I'm sure you fit into your old clothes by now. As little as you've come down to dinner lately, they might even be too big."

Georgina pulled the dress over her head and smiled slightly as she pulled the fabric forward, emphasizing the newly-acquired space between her body and the fabric.

She stared up at me angrily. "Are you happy? I'm dressed."

I took in a deep breath. There was a time I would have slapped a young lady across the face for daring to speak to me in such an audacious manner. I'd mellowed with age. "I don't take well to impertinent young ladies. You'll find I have little sympathy for the unmotivated. Both of my parents died before my fourteenth birthday. I took care of my younger siblings from that day forward. No one to wait on *me* hand and foot while I spent my days like the Queen of Sheba, propped on my feather pillows."

Georgina stood silently. The hate she felt for me oozed out of her and filled the room. It was of little concern. I'd won this kind of challenge with young girls twice as stubborn all my adult life.

"I'm out of bed. I'm wearing clothes. What else?" I took the brush from the dresser and began forcing it against her head, pulling it through her knotted, thick locks without mercy.

"Ow!" She flinched at an especially unforgiving section.

"You'll do this yourself tomorrow and you can be kinder to your head. Think of this pain as your incentive to become self-sufficient."

As soon as I'd finished, I took Georgina's long, curly hair and wrapped it up on top of her head, pinning things in place with pins I found in the dresser drawer.

"There!" I stood back, admiring my work. I spun Georgina around and pushed her forward. "Look in the mirror. A new you. Quite pleasant, wouldn't you agree, Francine?"

"Fine," Francine called from the hallway.

I hated to admit that, upon reflection, she looked like she had time traveled to the 1940s. The girl in the mirror more resembled my mother than a modern woman of 1975. Perhaps I enjoyed that just slightly.

Georgina glanced at the full-length mirror, her jaw dropping at the reflection she saw. The dress, at least six sizes too big, was multi-colored with a big bow at the chin. Her hair on top of her head was a style not common for anyone under fifty.

"Come now, I'll show you the garden and then we'll make lunch together."

We followed Francine and the baby downstairs, then continued past the cooing sounds and the baby smells and through the back door, where some old boots sat. "Put those on every time you work outside," I instructed. "They're to be left on the porch so we don't track dirt into Francine's clean house. At least it used to be clean." Georgina reluctantly pulled the boots over her feet, staring up at me when it was obvious her feet were far too large. I wore shoes too small for my feet for many years. Young people in this time had no idea what it was to struggle.

"You won't be wearing these to a fashion show," I snapped. "We'll find you some of Kenneth's old boots, or maybe Harlan's, if you feel you need more comfort. I wore the same pair of shoes until my toes came through the end as a child. A wise woman places necessity above comfort."

Georgina folded her arms across her chest but said nothing.

"See those nice, straight rows of green? Those are what we want to see clearly. See the green growing in between and willy-nilly? Those are weeds. Everything that isn't growing in an orderly fashion needs to go. Wait here a minute."

I walked toward the barn, leaving Georgina alone, outside for the first time in weeks. She tilted her face toward the sun and shut her eyes.

"Feels good, doesn't it? Sunshine and earth are the best remedies for whatever ails you," I commented upon return, remembering Kenneth scampering about in the garden while Francine and I pulled weeds. "Here you are." I handed her a pair of flowered gloves and a woven, floppy green hat.

"These may help ease your discomfort. I don't expect you to do them all today. And stay away from the strawberry patch."

Georgina looked at me helplessly.

I sighed. "Follow me." We walked to the far end of the garden, where a raised bed surrounded by brightly-painted rocks displayed four plants containing many clusters of leaves—three in each cluster, and small, white flowers.

Georgina scoffed. "Those don't look like any strawberries I've seen."

"Bend down closer." I pushed Georgina's head firmly. "See? Towards the bottom are some small, green berries. Your mother-in-law will come and trim back the runners a bit so the plants concentrate their energy on making big, juicy, red berries. Francine makes up her own name for her plants. It used to concern me, but we've all got our eccentricities. That one over there is a Purple Wonder, at least that's what she calls it. The woman makes up names for everything. Had a pepper plant once she called a Brownwell Beauty." I shook my head and glanced over at the door, where I knew she would be listening. "That doesn't make a lick of sense, Francine," I hollered. Even though she was a good wife for my Harlan and a dedicated mother to Kenneth, things she did often didn't add up properly in my head.

"Anyway, she uses those to make her special jam. Always wins the top prize at the fair. And right by your foot, that's the one she's hoping they'll name after her. She has to use special fertilizer and keep track of how much it gets watered. That's why she doesn't want anyone else messing with it. Those berries only come second to her boys in importance."

Georgina nodded. I could tell she felt no real interest.

"I painted those rocks for the garden, by the way. Colors I thought might be exciting to Kenneth." I chuckled to myself. "Don't think he cared much, but winter blues got the best of me one year, so I took up painting things. It was lucky my home included paneling on every wall or it would have become a nause-ating mix of blues and burnt orange. Oh, and the upturned boxes are covering weeds we want. Those are special dandelions. We'll cook the green ends with our supper soon. Hard to imagine a weed would be a part of our summer bounty, but nothing tastes better stir-fried with bacon grease and onions."

Back when I first started teaching school, it upset me when children seemed uninterested in the lessons. More than a few found themselves on the sorry end of my ruler. As the years went by, I concluded my job was to offer the information. It was up to them— lazy, ill-mannered, or attentive student—to decide if they would retain it. I still wasn't sure which category Kenneth's bride fell into.

"Okay. I'll pull all the weeds," Georgina replied, surprising me by her sudden turn.

"You don't do it all today. It's hard work. Just come out every day, do a little more. Soon you'll be ahead of the weeds and it won't take as much work. We'll add some mulch to keep the moisture in and cut down on the misery of plucking pesky plants in the hot sun. At the end of the summer, I'll teach you how to can all the produce. We'll have so much the kitchen will be over-flowing. Or maybe Francine will. That woman loves to can. Your mother-in-law would can my delicates if I'd let her."

I walked back into the house with a smile of satis-faction.

I'd given the girl an enormous task. I opened the kitchen curtain and watched, contemplating for a moment my next move if she decided to refuse my instructions when she thought I was out of sight. Most did not fare well when they tried.

Georgina picked up the hoe and paused for a moment before hacking at the weeds.

"Give her a little breathing room, Katherine," Francine insisted.

I busied myself preparing a glass of lemonade for each of us. "You want some, Francine?"

"I've got to head into town soon. My weekly rounds."

I kept my thoughts to myself. Never understood why the everyday nonsense of others was so important to her. When I glanced outside again, Georgina had already made a mess of things.

"That pile over there," I pointed to a healthy mass of green leaves and stalks, "those aren't weeds. You pulled out an entire row of beans. We won't tell Francine. I'll find you some seeds and you can replant them. It's spent so little time in the ground, I doubt she'll notice. They'll make fine mulch."

"Thank you," Georgina whispered. The lightness in her face from earlier was gone.

"Don't look sullen. Francine has no doubt pulled out a plant or two by accident. I'll find seeds right now. Stay here." Soon I reappeared with small seeds I placed in Georgina's hand. "Put these where the plants were. Cover them gently with soil, taking care to keep them in hill formation and then water them well with the hose. By the end of the summer, we won't even remember which plants were lost."

By the end of her first week of gardening, I caught her smiling when she finished an entire row of onions. Each day I found her resting on the grass for several minutes, arms splayed out like she was holding each blade in place. The look of peace on her face was enviable.

"Georgina, can you come here for a minute?" Francine called from the kitchen, where numerous boiling pots were producing meals for the harvest crew.

She laid her hoe down, took off her gloves, and stepped out of the extra-large boots Harlan donated. "Can you hold Kyan while I get ready to go?" She shoved the infant in Georgina's arms and walked into another room. Georgina hadn't held her son in weeks. I made her productive; I figured it was Francine's job to connect her to her son.

The infant squirmed in her arms and, for a moment, he looked like he might wiggle himself to the ground. I looked away.

"He likes it when you talk to him. Tell him about your day," Frannie said in passing. "We're going into town, Kyan and I. It's time for me to visit the courthouse and see a few people. Some friends have been asking to see my grandson." She stopped and turned abruptly. "You could come... if you want."

"No, I have more gardening to do. But thanks." Georgina tried smiling at Kyan. "Hi there. You might be a good little gardener. Once you get older, maybe you can help me," she continued awkwardly. "You'll be good at picking weeds..."

I stared at the two of them, mother and son. They didn't look anything alike. His features included a wide, flat face and a big nose. His dark hair touched the top of his shoulders, almost ready for a haircut that his grandmother was no doubt planning to document with a family dinner and endless photos.

"Ok, thanks, hon." Francine took Kyan from her arms and put him against her shoulder. "How's Grandma's big boy?" She patted his back. "Well, we'll be off now. Back in time for dinner. You've got things under control, Katherine?"

I motioned "go" with my hand. "There's not a banquet in the finest establishment I can't prepare on my own. Don't insult me by implying otherwise."

Georgina's face looked like a plateful of emotion. A young mother unable to connect with her son. It didn't come natural to some.

"Glass of tea to take out back with you?" I'd already poured one and set it on the counter.

"Yes, thanks." Georgina took her tea and headed back out to the garden.

I peered out the curtains as I always did, assuring myself she wasn't pulling any more plants. My insides tightened.

Chapter 17

Georgina

"HEY, GIGI!"

I was always daydreaming about him, about somehow leaving this farm and finding my way to San Francisco with or without Kyan. I jumped, not expecting anyone to be in my space. It still made my heart sing, that beautiful, perfect face, no matter what he'd done to me. I reached out and hugged him, an automatic response I regretted. He pulled me in close and we kissed passionately. Up my spine, down the front of me, an electrical current ran. I was dead and Edgar brought me back to life. Then I remembered where we were.

"What are you doing here, Edgar? I thought you went to San Francisco?" I wiped my lips with the back of my hand.

He looked down at the ground and put his hands in the pockets of his tight jeans. "That's what I told everybody. I took the money my mom and dad gave me to buy a crib and bought myself a new guitar. I was planning to take off for San Francisco after I emptied my savings. Boy, was my dad mad when I quit. He closed down my bank account."

I couldn't help but feel a little gleeful. "Oh, really?"

"Yeah, probably shouldn't have bought the guitar before I left. But I already told the old man I was leaving and they wouldn't allow me back in the house to get the other one." Edgar flipped his long hair, one of many things on the long list of things that always drove me wild. The scent of *Manly* drifted to my nostrils in the mid-afternoon breeze. "I've been hanging out with friends. On their couches. Far as my folks know, I'm already groovin' in San Francisco."

"Oh?"

"That's why I'm here. I... I need some cash. Gotta boogie to San Francisco pretty soon. I don't want them to see me and think I couldn't make it on my own."

My eyes narrowed. "Do you think I have money? I'm hoeing weeds in somebody else's garden. I don't have anything."

"Well, you have access. Rich people always have something expensive lying around."

I thought about Frannie's frugality. And her kindness. "You're crazy! I'm not stealing from my in-laws."

"Geeky dude Kenneth? You're not married to him. You're married to me. Have you told them the kid's mine yet?"

Anger welled up inside me. "I can't believe you... how did you even get in here?"

"The big gate's open. Some gomer told me they always leave it open during harvest. I didn't want to take any chances, though, so I found a fence I could climb over. You can't hide from me, Gigi."

My throat began to close and sweat formed on my brow. I could run inside, but he would probably follow. How would Katherine react when he told her?

"Y'know, you could probably come with me. You take enough money and we could go together, just like we planned. Might have to leave the kid behind. What's its name?"

"Kyan. HIS name is Kyan." There was a tingle of excitement. He still wanted me. I could still go, just like I dreamt, even though it was wrong in every way.

"Hmm. Dumb name. Still think you should've named him after a band. Aerosmith, maybe."

"How long do I have until you tell them? I mean, it's blackmail, right?"

His eyes widened. "That's a crazy hostile word. You're just helping a friend, ya dig? I'll come back in a week. That's how long I figure I can hide from my parents. I'll meet you back here. Don't worry, I'll be careful so your doofus 'husband' doesn't see me." He winked. "I can't get over it. You've got a good scam going here, Gigi."

My face, minutes ago full of peace, was now ashen. "I don't understand how I'll..."

"Never seemed to have any problems working the system when you lived with your parents. You'll figure something out."

Chapter 18

Kenneth

MOM REMINDED ME to give her time. "Having a baby takes a lot out of you, Ken," she said. Mom always knew what was best, but I got to thinking, maybe she didn't understand how important it was that Gigi come to love me as much as I loved her.

She said from the first minute she saw Dad, she knew he was the right and only one for her. She told me to trust myself and allow that feeling to come. That's how I knew, when I saw Gigi for the first time, that she was right for me. Everything in my body told me it was.

"You're sure, son?" Mom asked.

I looked her in the eye, like she told me to do when I meant business. "More'n anything I've ever known to be true."

"I trust your judgement, Kenneth. I raised a smart boy. I'll do whatever I can to help the process along."

It seemed like each week she got prettier. She let her hair grow past her shoulders and pulled it back with a big barrette. When she smiled, her eyes sparkled. Looked like someone straight out of a magazine. When she couldn't talk to me, she always winked as she walked by, letting me know I was still part of her world.

After freshman year, when everyone was making fun of me, Gigi sat by me at lunch, at least on Tuesdays when her friends were in the extended hour home ec class. I didn't mind being by myself, but she said a guy like me looked like he needed companionship.

We talked about most everything. She told me about her brothers, how they drove her nuts. She talked about her mom and said she wished they were closer. I pretty much just listened, deciding that it was her needing the companionship more than me.

Some days she didn't talk to me if she was surrounded by lots of friends. That's okay. I understood why. I'm not popular and not handsome, at least not in the way Mom would make it seem. Mom says, "The world would move just fine without more attractive people. It's the kind ones who are always in short supply."

When she started dating Edgar Pepper, she became a completely different person. She'd dated lots of guys in our class before. All of them were dumber than her. I could see she was just killing time, trying to decide what was coming next. But with Edgar, dumb as he was, he cast a spell on her.

It didn't matter how many fart jokes he told or bra straps he snapped as he walked down the hall. Every-thing he did made my poor, innocent Gigi swoon. She couldn't see what I saw, that she was losing herself in a person who was an empty pit. If someone didn't rescue her soon, she would be trapped at the bottom with no way out.

That's why I went to the party. Mom told me all about Edgar, like she did all the kids in my class.

Said she didn't want me to have any surprises. "If you love that girl, get her out of his clutches," she instructed. Mom helped me pick out the right outfit and told me I didn't have to worry about coming home late that night.

I wasn't expecting to conceive our first child that night. A gentleman would never ask that of a lady before marriage. But I couldn't let her suffer or fall into someone else's hands when she was in that state.

I came home and told Mom right away. She wasn't mad. "Oh, Ken," she said with a little sadness. "I wanted something different for you." But she understood.

When Gigi told me she was pregnant, Mom said we had to make sure our baby had a good life. She put a hand on each side of my face, the way she always did when she wanted me to hear something important. "I'll take care of everything, Ken," she said. I knew she would.

'Fore long, I heard about Lost in Pepperville getting all these... gigs, is what they called them. The posters were up all over school. I saw some in the back of Mom's car, figured she'd been doing the neighborly thing and helping young kids get their start. Edgar was out every night, leaving poor Gigi alone.

Chapter 19

Georgina

KATHERINE INSTRUCTED ME to go to the barn and take the grass clippings Kenneth had been collecting and carry as much as I could in the wheelbarrow to the garden. I spread it carefully around each plant to keep the moisture in the and weeds down, just the way she wanted.

All the rows of beans, peas, onions, peppers, and watermelon had been weeded. All that was left was the lettuce. And Frannie's special berries. I couldn't wait to show Katherine the result of my hard work. On my way into the house, Frannie met me at the door. Kyan was gurgling happily in her arms.

"I was just coming to get you. I was thinking we should go into town and get you some new clothes. Your old things don't really fit you that well anymore. Maybe a fancy pair of bell-bottoms too?"

I smiled. "Sure. I'd like that. Oh, Frannie, I was wondering about your strawberries. Katherine said not to weed them, but..."

"Don't touch those!" Frannie's voice rose. Kyan, startled by her sudden change of demeanor, began to fuss. "It's all right, my sweet boy. Granny didn't mean to scare you." She pressed the top of his head to her lips and kissed him. He grabbed at her lips and she took his hand and put it on her cheek.

These displays of affection were starting to make me uncomfortable. I wasn't sure why. Occasionally, Frannie would lay Kyan on a quilted, wheat-colored blanket on the living room floor. Sometimes I would sit beside him, trying to decide how to talk to him. Once, I put my hand on his stomach, just to feel him breathe. Frannie always scooped him up before we spent much time together.

"I've been growing berries since we lived on Lecher Farm. Used to have my own little patch there on a raised bit of garden. It was my little piece of heaven. The work was so hard, it was my escape. I'd sit and talk to them when I finished weeding. These little wonders have a short life in the ground, so it's all about what you give while they're here. The more attention given, the more they reward you with sweet berries. After three years' time, the plant has given all it has to give and you start over, nurturing something new. I thank them for all they've given me before putting them in the compost pile."

Her fervor scared me a bit. "Sounds nice," I replied awkwardly. Frannie only spoke passionately

about Kenneth, Kyan, and now her strawberries.

"I've got special fertilizer made of fish something-or-other and I have to keep track of how much I water and weed for the university." She beamed, standing a bit taller.

"I'm positive they'll name P90834 after me. Did I tell you that? Yes, I'm sure I did. The Franniebell berry will be my legacy. I don't think you've sampled my jam yet. Good heavens, I wonder why I haven't shared. Wait a minute."

She returned to the living room, where I sat tickling Kyan's feet, and handed me a half-piece of bread smeared with a thick, red jam. "Here, try this. The best you'll ever taste."

The sweet jam included a slight hint of something hot. I wrinkled my brow, trying to figure out exactly why jam would have such a kick.

"You're wondering about my secret ingredients? I view my jam as my scrapbook. It contains all my blood, sweat, and tears along with a few secrets. I've tweaked it over the years." Her voice wavered slightly. "It's my stamp on the world. It's what says, 'Frannie Brownwell was here.' Next to my Kenneth, of course."

Now I understood. It was the only thing on this huge property that belonged only to Frannie. "I won't touch them. I promise."

Frannie smiled. "That's a good girl. Now run and change out of your garden clothes and we'll head into town."

Frannie strapped Kyan into his car seat, something I found completely ridiculous. Both of my brothers sat on the laps of other occupants of the car and it worked out just fine. But Frannie insisted, saying it was the latest in car safety.

I hadn't been into town since giving birth. Things seemed louder and unfamiliar. The bustling Main Street area, where I spent my summer days half watching my brothers play hide-and-seek between the trees while I gossiped with my friends about the latest fashion faux pas of underclassmen, was full of the new crop of teens.

I felt a small pang of sadness. Those days of innocence were gone. I wondered what happened to the girls who used to envy me, who might be heading to college soon. We pulled up in front of Sage's Department Store.

I stood beside the car, staring at the area where the other teens were gathered. Some of the girls were giggling, most likely about me, the town pariah. I stared down at my clothes—a baggy pair of flowered pants and a wrinkled t-shirt. Just last year, every girl in the senior class came to school with yellow-dyed tops days after I unknowingly wore a mustard-stained shirt in all my afternoon classes.

"C' mon, hon. We've got lots to do." Frannie hoisted Kyan on one shoulder and her purse on the other.

I tried on several outfits, pleased by how nice I looked in the mirror. My arms were starting to feel muscular from my gardening work. I could see my waist again. Though the store clerk seemed uncomfortable helping us, she was polite to Frannie.

"Do you want a large bag, or do you want your 'ward'

to carry them in a box?" she asked with a disapproving sniff.

Frannie, though fuming, took a controlled breath. "Georgina is my daughter-in-law. I'll thank you to keep your nasty attitude to yourself. I know your mother well and she wouldn't be happy to hear about your late-night adventures with the pharmacist. Georgina, take your things and we'll be off."

By now it should have seemed normal. The stares, the attitude. A few months of blissful isolation temporarily erased the hurt. It came back in a rush. "Thank you, Frannie."

"One thing you need to remember about me—I know everything that happens in this town. EVERY-THING. It is my most powerful weapon."

Katherine mentioned a few times that Frannie possessed "strange hobbies". Gossip must have been one of them.

We walked down the block slowly, neither of us wanting to leave the warm sun. "You could use some new shoes. Would you be opposed to stopping at the shoe store?"

We paused and looked at each other. I hadn't seen my father since I left home. He was just as adamant as Mildred that I wasn't a part of their family anymore.

"You have every right to wear shoes. Your feet didn't do anything wrong."

We burst out laughing. "Okay, I guess you're right. But I don't know if my dad will wait on us. If that happens, can we leave?"

Frannie nodded. I opened the door to Shoe Shangri-la and we both stepped inside. My stomach immediately twisted when I saw my father waiting on a customer.

Mavis, the other store employee, came over to greet us. "Georgina! I heard you'd left town with..." She turned red when she realized she had temporarily forgotten the rest of the story. "Oh, dear. Can I help you with something?"

I stared at the rows of shoes on the wall. I was seldom in the store. My father generally brought home shoes that had been on sale so long they served no further purpose in his inventory. I always found a way to squeeze my feet into them, no matter the size.

"I'll try on..."

"No. We'll wait for Mr. Hardwick. Thank you," Frannie replied curtly.

I frowned and shook my head.

"Well, if you think that's wise, I'll go get him." Mavis turned abruptly and went to the other side of the store, where she whispered into the ear of the store manager. Turning his stony face toward his new customers, he paused to glare at me. It was meant to bore a hole through me and leave me lifeless, right where I stood. It was working.

"He'll wait on us or I'll never come in this store again," Frannie announced in her "come to supper" voice. The other customer began playing with her hair, swirling the ends furiously in her hand.

Bob set brown, leather clogs beside his other customer and came to my side. He straightened his tie and ignored his only daughter. His familiar, musky smell made me ache for home.

"What can I help you with, Mrs. Brownwell?" he asked tersely.

"You can measure your daughter's foot and help her find some shoes." Frannie was still speaking in a voice too loud for the space. Kyan began to fuss. "Now there, Grandson, Don't let your grandfather scare you. He can't hurt you while I'm here."

"Sit here." Bob pointed to the nearest chair, ignoring Frannie. He yanked off my shoe as if it were covered in dung and shoved my foot into his shoe measuring device. "Nine-and-a-half." We sat for a moment in silence, daring the other to speak. "Well?" he snapped. "I don't have time for indecision. There has to be something you've found."

Now that I was outside so much, when I was feeling down, I could cry or scream or whatever I needed until the feelings were gone. But today, I pushed all the emotion away. Tears would only make me appear weak to my father, just what he wanted.

"I have three picked out. Maybe more."

Frannie came over and stood beside Bob, rocking Kyan back and forth. "Get a pair of garden shoes, hon. And a couple more."

I nodded, staring intently at my foot, not wanting him to see my joy and try and take it away.

Someone finally thought I deserved to have shoes that fit, of my own choosing.

Frannie cleared her throat. "Make sure you give her whatever she wants. I would hate to have to make public what I know about the missing receipts from some months ago."

I looked at him, shocked. That wasn't the Bob Hardwick I knew.

Bob blinked fast. He pushed the corners of his mouth in but said nothing.

When I found the perfect-fitting sensible shoes I needed for the garden and a pair of boots that zipped up the side of my calf, I handed them to my father.

"Oh, dear. Kyan has made quite a mess of his pants. I'm going to take him back to the car and get him cleaned up." There was a foul-smelling substance oozing from the bottom of his blue corduroy overalls. Frannie was trying to keep it contained within his blanket, but some was already dripping on the floor.

"Mavis! Get the cleaning supplies!" Beads of sweat were forming on his wide forehead.

Frannie handed me her purse. "You pay for your shoes and I'll meet you back at the car."

I looked at her helplessly. I had power as long as Frannie was standing there. By myself, I wasn't sure how to handle Bob Hardwick. Frannie squeezed my arm and walked out.

As Mavis cleaned up the floor, Bob rang up the shoes, taking care to write out a detailed receipt.

"That would be your offspring then?"

"Yes, that's Kyan. He's a really good baby. He hardly ever cries." I summoned the courage to look at his face. The same stern man I lived with for seventeen years. Same wrinkles, receding hairline, and flaring nostrils.

"That will be $54.50." Bob stared at the counter, tapping his fingers impatiently.

I opened Frannie's wallet, thinking about Edgar's

threat. It would be so easy to take something now. She would never know. "Here." I handed him sixty dollars.

"You broke your mother's heart," he sighed. "Your mother's best friend, Shirleen left in the middle of junior year, didn't even tell your mother she wouldn't be coming back. Poor Mildred was left trying to fight off the bullies by herself. Without someone to protect her, she was severely injured and spent several months in the hospital with broken bones. Missed her senior year entirely."

"What does that have to do with me?"

"You've similarly abandoned her because of your weak countenance."

There was nothing I could say, and I didn't want to give him the satisfaction of knowing I felt bad. My heart had just begun to heal and I didn't want it to fracture again. "Tell Mom... tell Mom... Can I have my change, please?"

I took the change and put it all back in Frannie's wallet. I needed to say something to show I was just as strong as he was. "Thank you for waiting on me, Mr. Hardwick. Please tell your boys I miss them." I turned around abruptly and left without waiting for a reply.

Leaving Shoe Shan-gri-la, I held my head just a little higher. I felt a strength that hadn't existed before today. It lasted exactly one block until I reached the car and realized I still hadn't figured out how to pay Edgar. He would demand that I give him something.

Luckily, Frannie was quick with a washcloth, cleaning

up most of Kyan's mess by the time I got to the car. She kept extra clothes in the trunk for just such occasions. Kyan was sitting in his car seat, happily gnawing on the rubber ducky Kenneth gave him. "Did you get everything you needed?" she asked innocently.

"I did. Thank you." I handed Frannie her purse and sat down in the back seat. "Did you want me to see my father?"

"Well, hon, you've been a mess for a while. I was thinking you might want to see someone in your family. No matter how hurtful, sometimes we just need to get things out of our system before we can move on and start making it right."

"I did. Get things out of my system. Thank you." "I feel like ice cream, don't you?" Frannie smiled. "I'm sure Kyan would like to try some too."

We drove to the Dairy Barn, the only drive-thru window in town. Frannie spooned a small bit of the creamy goodness into his mouth. His eyes got wide and he began flapping his arms up and down, as if propelling himself forward to the dish in front of his grandmother. Both of us Brownwell women laughed until we cried. All the way home we talked about who would act out Kyan's reaction for the rest of the family.

Frannie went in to put Kyan down for his nap. I changed my clothes, slipping on my new gardening shoes. I decided I would do more weeding, despite the heat and the fact I had taken care of most of the weeds. It was my best place to think. On a whim, I searched through my school supplies box and found my camera.

Katherine, who had been sitting with a book on her

large chest in the rocker, stirred as I walked by. "I'm not sleeping, if that's what you're thinking." She sat up in the chair and adjusted first her hair and then the lopsidedness of her chest.

"Okay," I chuckled. "I'm going to go out and garden."

"When the boys came in earlier, they said they need a tool kit. Since Frannie needs to run to enter her jam in the fair for judging, you can take the little dirt bike motorcycle with the toolbox strapped on the back."

I felt panicky. "I've never done that."

"Then you'll do a new thing today. I'll help you get loaded up." Katherine quickly guided me out the door, giving me no time to think of a reasonable excuse not to go.

She strapped the toolbox on the back of the faded red bike and handed me the key. "It's very simple. Turn the key and kick start it and you're ready. Just go slow."

I held back tears. "Where am I going? I don't even know."

"Drive down the main road until you see the sign that says Johnson Farm. Turn left there, go another quarter mile, and take a left at the dead oak. You'll see the old barn there. Nothing to it."

I nodded, though I really wasn't sure of myself. Once I was moving, feeling the wind caressing my hair, I felt a sense of exhilaration. Having never had a driver's license, it was the closest thing I'd experienced to complete freedom.

Instead of Kenneth, Harlan was waiting in the barn when I arrived. "Frannie's got you on the motorcycle now? It's about time you was treated like family."

I handed him the tools and smiled, at once proud of myself and feeling foolish for taking pride in something so simple. "I can bring anything you need. I have lots of time."

Harlan nodded. "Did Frannie tell you 'bout those eggs you ate this morning?" I shook my head.

"They were Friday eggs. Even though it's Tuesday." He winked.

"Friday eggs on a Tuesday. You can't get those just anywhere in Pepperville." I felt good, being included in the family joke.

After dropping off the tools, I paused when I reached the crossroad. Instead of turning right to head back to the main house, I turned left, toward Spud Hill. I got off the motorcycle and caught my breath. It was beautiful here, almost more beautiful than the garden area. The entire farm was visible from this hilltop. I laid down on the ground and closed my eyes. It was a peace I began to relish, this farm life.

The perfect picnic on top of this hill, the breeze blowing through my hair as I nibble on a sandwich made with Frannie's special jam. Just me and...

Suddenly I heard an approaching vehicle. Maybe Kenneth had come to surprise me. It was time I put effort into getting to know my husband.

Instead, when I sat up, I saw Edgar's car. I gulped.

"I didn't think you were coming back for a while."

"Just driving by, y'know, and the gate was still open, so it seemed like a good idea to check." He slammed his car door shut and came over close to me. "Did you find something valuable?"

"Not yet. I'm looking though..." I didn't have time

to ask why he would casually drive by a farm miles from town.

"Gigi, I gotta get out of town. Don't make this harder than it needs to be. Just go into that chick's bedroom and take something. She's gotta have jewels laying around."

The idea of Frannie with jewelry was hysterical. "Not Kenneth's mom. Not ever. Honestly, I don't know what you want me to take."

"You'll think of something. Maybe they have something valuable in that big barn."

Impulsively I threw my arms around his neck and began kissing him. I unbuttoned his shirt and he caught my hand with his. "Won't somebody see us?"

"Let's go in your car." The door to his Superbird swung open, just like old times. I began unbuttoning my shirt and he kissed my shoulders, down to my chest. It felt right, at least at first. Our same old rhythm, like we were still in the middle of our senior year. I held his face, looking into his eyes, the way I did after every other time we'd been together. I didn't have the usual rush of affection. He was becoming something of a stranger the more months we spent apart.

"Is this good enough? Will you go after we're done?" I knew it wasn't.

"Do you think I can get an apartment in San Francisco on *that*? Geez, girl." Edgar pushed me to the side and got out of the car. He pulled cigarettes out of his back pocket and put one in his mouth. His open shirt was blowing in the breeze as he surveyed the land.

I buttoned my shirt, staring at him longingly. I both desired and despised him. And more than anything, I felt dirty.

"Sure is lonely out here. It would drive me crazy."

"When did you start smoking?" I got out of the back seat and smoothed my blouse.

"When I realized I didn't exist anymore to my parents."

He had no idea. "It doesn't make any sense for you to be here. I have nothing for you. Don't come back, okay?"

"Oh, I'll be back. Next time, you're not gettin' a piece of Edgar first." He winked. "I mean it. This is it, Gigi. Or I'll make a big deal about that kid bein' mine. I'll tell them I want the kid and cause a ruckus.

Man, that will get ugly for you."

The idea of where we were standing and the possibility it offered popped into my head. I pushed that idea right out of my head, at least for now.

Chapter 20

Georgina

THE NIGHTS KENNETH and Harlan got home after dark, I enjoyed eating with Katherine and Frannie. There was an ease that came with just us three women preparing meals and eating them in the kitchen instead of at the big, formal table.

"Georgina's got your garden in tip-top shape, Francine. It looks like you've got enough ripe berries to work on your jam." Katherine stacked our plates and began scrubbing the giant, stainless steel pot in the sink.

Frannie tipped her head back to see if Kyan was still asleep on her shoulder. "I'm just going to lay him down, hold on." She stood up and started to walk out of the kitchen, but then paused. "Do you want to kiss him goodnight?"

I stood up quickly and kissed Kyan's dark head. He smelled like Frannie's homemade lilac soap. "Good night, son," I said, not as uncomfortably as I had the previous week. He stirred just slightly.

When Frannie returned, she was wearing her big, fuzzy blue slippers and matching robe. "Can you make me some tea, Katherine?" She sat back in her chair with a thud.

"So unlike you," Katherine remarked, setting the kettle on the stove. "I don't believe I've ever seen you in your night clothes before."

"I'm just exhausted. I'm not used to having a little one around during harvest. Not for many years." She smiled. "Where were we? Strawberries."

"I'll pick them for you!" I volunteered. I loved spending time in the garden by myself. Frannie relented, allowing me to weed the berries earlier in the week because she didn't have time between taking care of Kyan and preparing for the fair.

"Proceed with caution, Gigi," she lectured. "They must be tended to with extreme care. My special berries require extra attention."

I was happy on the farm during those hours. I'd begun photographing the plants from ground level, taking pictures of the juicy berries up close. The Franniebells were distinct, with a point at the bottom that made them appear heart-shaped. There were only a few berries on the plants, unlike the Purple Wonder plants that were heavy with fruit. I didn't want to mention this to Frannie when she was so tired. "I mean, I can look them over and tell you which plants are ready at least."

"Well, I don't know. They have to be picked just so. Berries must be *severed* from the plant at the stem, and then you gently twist them between your fingers and pull lightly. You don't want to pull too hard or you might damage the plant. I have a special padded bag I place inside a basket to pick them so they aren't bruised. They aren't as easy to pick as, say, a pepper or a pea."

Katherine set a cup of tea in front of Frannie. "Good heavens, it isn't like she's asking to build the next spacecraft in the barn. You're sitting here in your unmentionables, too exhausted to dress appropriately. Don't you think you should delegate some of your tasks? Let the girl do the work and then you can teach her how to make your famous jam. She's offering you a favor. Take it."

Frannie stared at me with bloodshot eyes. "I suppose you're right. But I will need to see the first batch you bring in, just to make sure they haven't been bruised or damaged. And don't pick the berries from P90834. I'll need to photograph those to send to the university. When they become the famous Franniebell, I want a picture of the first product framed and hanging on our wall."

Katherine and I looked at each other and chuckled. She and I were developing a respect for our two different worlds. I could only imagine what she'd thought of me; pregnant and alone at seventeen. "Your produce is second to none, Francine. Wait 'til you see the awards she wins at the fair. Her jam is the pride of the county."

"First place, ten years and counting," Frannie announced with satisfaction. "I'm going to head to bed now. Kyan will be up at 4:00 a.m., no matter how tired I am. Goodnight, ladies."

I decided not to mention the up-close shots until I

had a chance to get them developed. It would be a nice surprise.

Something weighed heavily on my mind since my last meeting with Edgar. Katherine was the only person I could talk to about delicate matters with discretion.

"Ma'am, can I ask you something?"

"Questions, unless impertinent, always lead to wisdom," Katherine replied, taking a sip of her tea. "And the time of familial recognition has come. You may call me Aunt Katherine."

"Aunt Katherine, I've always thought... been told, I guess... that you can only get pregnant by the person you love. Is that true?"

Katherine folded her arms and sat back in her chair. "What an interesting question. My studies of biology..." she paused and glanced at my confused face. I didn't know if Kenneth explained that he had done most of my homework.

"There is a question of pregnancy and then a question of fatherhood. The two answers can be quite different."

"I don't understand."

"A young woman who finds herself in the family way may decide in her own mind the parentage of the child. But that answer may differ from the person she knows to be the real father figure to her child. It's all up to the young woman to decide if these two titles are to be bestowed on the same individual."

I nodded. I was still unsure of Edgar and what he might do. But I trusted Katherine.

Katherine stood up and patted my shoulder. "I'm

glad you came to me with that question. Francine has too much on her mind for these kinds of concerns. Goodnight, Georgina."

Kenneth knocked on my door every night when he got home. Though he was tired and his body ached, he wanted a connection with me. He could see I was bonding more with his mother and aunt than with him.

"I just want to talk, Gigi," he pleaded.

"Maybe tomorrow," I always said, feeling a twinge of guilt. It was so much easier to immerse myself in the horror series *The Bones of Jonas Milkwork* than actually deal with Kenneth. How could I look him in the eye when I had been with Edgar in the back of his car? When I was plotting how I could steal from his family, who had been nothing but kind? Kenneth deserved so much better.

I was digging through the closet in my room, trying to find something of value to give Edgar, when I found the boxed set. There were many containers of Kenneth's things from childhood: pictures, clothing, and mementos from every school performance. Nothing that would seem valuable enough to Edgar that he would leave me alone.

Sometimes I imagined what it must've been like to be so treasured. Kenneth's every move was documented by Frannie. To be the center of his parents' world must've felt wonderful.

"You can come in," I replied quietly one night.

Kenneth was still wearing his work clothing, a tattered black t-shirt and dirty jeans. He wasn't bad looking. His long, lean body would have been appealing to an ordinary girl in my class. His face was beginning to feel familiar, comforting.

"Oh, you found my books," he commented, pointing to the boxes on my bed. "I loved those. Read them twice."

"I really like to read. I never really had time when I was out partying every night with Edgar," I said before I realized I'd said his name. "Sorry."

"That's okay. I can't erase him. Wish you could see him the way I do."

I looked at the floor. I couldn't get him out of my head. Even when I hadn't seen him for months, the minute I smelled his smell, tasted his lips, and touched his hair I was under his spell again. It was wrong and I knew it.

I thought about Frannie, how Kenneth was her world. I owed something to Frannie. "Kenneth, you're a great guy. The best. Probably better than Edgar." I smiled the fake smile, the one I perfected when I was trying to convince my parents I would be going straight to bed.

"Thanks, Gigi. That means a lot." He moved closer, trying to kiss me. Automatically, I turned my head away. "I'm so tired tonight. All of this heat is getting to me," I said quickly. As an afterthought, I kissed him on the cheek. For Frannie.

"I understand."

That night I fell asleep fantasizing about Edgar. The three of us, together in San Francisco. I pushed it out of my mind for so long, it was thrilling to hope that dream might become a reality. That was what I wanted more than anything, even if it meant hurting this new family, if I was being honest.

"There are four species of monkeys in Costa Rica. Can you imagine? Sure woulda thought there was just one kind, like on the animal show we see on Sunday nights." Kenneth always brought new facts to the dinner table, no matter how tired he was from his day in the field. I appreciated that Kenneth was so smart. Smarter than Edgar, I had to admit. He read the encyclopedias stored in the informal living room, just for fun.

"Harlan, did you hear your son? He's found different types of monkeys." Frannie nudged her half-asleep husband.

"Hmm? Of course, dear."

"What else did you learn, Kenneth? Tell your wife what you read last night." Frannie winked at me. I smiled back at her uncomfortably.

Kenneth leaned back in his chair and clasped his hands behind his head. "Well, this ain't from the encyclopedia, but you know those video games they have at the gas station?"

I remembered the times Edgar and I would go in there to make out and laugh at the geeks who spent their spare time wasting their quarters on games. When Edgar played, he always begged one of them to "loan" him a few quarters. I posed seductively on the side of the machine as I watched, the way the actresses did in all the best movies.

"I've been there a couple of times," I replied. I hoped Kenneth hadn't been one of the people we laughed about in Edgar's car right before we had sex.

"They got a new one. It's called *Gunslinger*. You try to shoot your rival before he takes your girlfriend. I got the high score on it three times in a row now."

"That's my boy. Always the best in all that you do." Frannie got up from the table and kissed the top of his head, the way I kissed Kyan.

"What're you doin' in the gas station? That's not where a married man should be spendin' his time," Harlan scolded.

"I only stop when I'm needin' gas, really, Dad. I don't neglect my—"

"It's okay, really," I interjected. "Kenneth can play Gun-Whatever if he wants." I stood and began collecting plates. "He's just fine." I hurriedly made my way to the kitchen. "I trust him and, if he wants to have some fun, he should."

"You're a keeper," Harlan called after me.

I gulped as I scraped the plates into the pile of scraps accumulated for the barn cats. I was glad no one could see the burning red of my cheeks.

That night, I knocked on Kenneth's door. When he opened it, he was dressed in red-and-grey striped pajamas, just like my brothers had worn. I noticed his face had become tanned from his hours outside. His arms were developing muscles too. Nothing like Edgar's but more impressive than they looked during the school year. "Gigi? Is everything okay?"

"Everything's fine. I just... I don't know." I turned to walk away. *What was I doing? Didn't I love Edgar?*

"Wait!" I could tell he wanted to touch me. I knew

his mind almost as well as I knew my own from our years of non-togetherness during school, when I so callously ignored every single one of his needs.

"You must've come here for something. I've got lots more books in my room. I've read them all several times. You could look through them, maybe find something you like?"

I sighed. "Okay, sure." I walked into Kenneth's room, one that mirrored the one I was sleeping in. It was neat and sparsely furnished. His bed sported a homemade green-and-brown quilt with the words "Beloved Son" stitched on the middle square. I plopped down on the quilt. It was strange to be in the bedroom of my husband for the first time in our marriage. I didn't feel married.

"What do you do for fun, Ken?" I laid back on the bed, staring at the popcorn texture on the ceiling.

"What do you mean? Between farm work and school... I... Sorry, I didn't mean to bring up school. But that didn't give me much extra time. Glad it's done. But now that it *is* done, I read. And our boy, I like to spend time with him too."

I remembered my former life. Babysitting my brothers and going to parties was all I had. And yet it filled my mind and all my days. No, that wasn't true. Edgar filled my mind.

"Kenneth? Do you think about what you might have done? If we didn't have Kyan?"

Kenneth frowned. "What do you mean? Like, are you asking if I would have married someone else? I've always been in love with you, Gigi. There's no one else for me."

"No, not that. I mean, what you might be doing now that you've graduated. Would you be doing something different? Maybe going to college? You're so smart."

Kenneth sat down beside me and leaned closer for a minute before sitting upright. "I was always gonna farm with Dad. This is our place. We're building it together. When my dad took over, a lot of good farm ground was just going to waste. We've got the equipment, and now we've got corn and wheat and maybe next year we'll have—"

"No, Kenneth. You're not getting what I'm saying." I was exasperated, but how could someone so content in their world understand? "Maybe there's more out in the world besides this farm. Have you thought about that? New cities to see and probably exciting people to meet."

"This is all the excitement I need. I'm gonna be running this place one day. Me and my son. It'll be a lot of work for you too." He smiled. "You and Mom will have your hands full."

An idea popped into my head. "You and your dad bought lots of equipment? I bet it was expensive."

"Yeah, Dad's been workin' on it since I was little. You should see the big barn, it's full of nice tools and..."

"I'm tired, Ken. Do you have those books?"

He handed me another boxed set, this time containing *The Chronicles of Bluth and Chandler*.

"Thanks."

I kissed him once more on the cheek. Each time it became easier, more comfortable. He was soft and inviting, despite not being connected to Edgar. I headed back to my bedroom. At least now I had another idea.

Chapter 21

Georgina

"THIS *HAS* TO be it." I pressed my mouth against Edgar's, running my fingers through his long hair one last time. I could feel his heart, beating hard in his bare chest next to mine. I hadn't meant for us to be touching each other on Brownwell property again, but he kissed my neck before I could get the words out.

We agreed to meet once more at the same spot on Spud Hill. Bringing something to the south barn for Kenneth and Harlan had become a daily occurrence. I loved taking the little motorcycle around the farm, surveying the golden fields of wheat and tall green corn.

He began removing my two-tone, green-striped shirt —the one Frannie bought for me on one of her weekly trips to town. The old Georgina slipped into submission for a moment, ready to allow him to do whatever he needed. Then I remembered why we were here in the first place and pushed his hands away. "Here, I brought you this." I handed him the wrench set I found in the barn.

"What am I supposed to do with that?"

"There's a whole barn full of these. I can't imagine they would miss them. Take it and sell it to another farmer. I'll get you more." I combed through my hair with my fingers. I was starting to feel like my old self again.

Edgar grabbed my arm. "Gigi, you don't get it. I need something *big*. I'm gonna make a move to the city. Something, like the price of a car. Like the price of *my* car. I need to find a place to live and eat while my career is getting off the ground. These dirt farmers have to have something lying around you can take."

The words were a punch in the gut. In that moment, I realized my touch meant nothing to him. He was supposed to be overcome with desire. To want me more than any material item. His only focus was stealing— getting *me* to steal—from good people. "I don't have anything, Edgar. I'm pretty much useless out here. I can get you corn, or lettuce, or maybe even a few strawberries. That's all I've got. I don't know what you think I can do."

He pushed his t-shirt down, prematurely hiked in anticipation of a dance that had long-since ended. "How do you think we're going together if you don't have any money? I can't have you dragging on me, just being extra weight. Do you understand?"

I nodded. Even though I dreamt of him, I felt so worthless every time I saw him. The small things I did on the farm didn't mean anything in the real world. He made sure I knew it.

"Maybe I shouldn't go then." It slipped out before I could correct myself. "Maybe I shouldn't," I said again. The second time it hit me. *Maybe, deep down, I didn't really want to go.* "I don't think we could be together every day. It didn't work before." I liked him even less now. I actually *liked* life on the farm. "I've got things I'm doing here. I've got this garden I'm working on and we're canning everything for the winter. And I'm working on things with Kyan. He reaches out for me now when he sees me."

"Who's... oh, yeah... the kid. Never thought you were really going, to be honest. You seem like you belong here." Edgar's face was twisted in a smirk. "Just because you can't go doesn't mean you don't have to help me though. They've gotta have something of value. You've been messing with me like I'm your parents. You don't think I see what you're doing? I'm coming back in two days and I'm gonna sit down with the whole family and tell them how you've been playing them. I can't believe ole Kenny hasn't already figured this one out. School smarts ain't everything, huh?" Edgar smiled his million-dollar smile.

My entire body tensed. "Don't make fun of Kenneth. He's a good guy. He's a good *man*. He's been trying to make a life for—"

"He's a simpleton who won't ever do anything important. I'm going to make a name for myself. By this time next year, he'll still be stumbling around in his dung-covered boots. I'll be headlining the big clubs."

It sounded absurd. It was absurd. Why hadn't I realized that before?

"He's building this farm into one of the biggest

producers in the state. That's something. They took this land from almost nothing and have turned a profit."

"*Blah, blah, blah*. You've changed, babe. You used to be interesting." Edgar shook his hair. "I could tell from the first time I saw you out here, covered in dirt, that you were turning into something weird. Some kind of Kenneth clone. If Old Gigi could hear you, she'd be shocked."

I gulped. "You don't know what I've been through. I had a baby, all by myself. After you dumped me, I didn't know where I would go. But Kenneth's family took me in and made me feel like I belonged."

Yes, I thought, *I did belong*—for the first time in my life. It was completely different from high school, where the females who surrounded me were there to somehow absorb my status or meet my boyfriend. Those nights in the kitchen with Katherine and Frannie, talking about our long days, I was one of them.

Edgar snickered. "You don't have it so bad. I'm sleeping on Theo's couch until I have to move to Larry's couch. My parents won't talk to me and my dad shut down my bank account, so I can't even get to San Francisco like I planned. All because you went and got pregnant." He clenched his fists. "You ruined my life."

I got out of the car and slammed the door. An anger was swelling in me that I hadn't realized existed. I bent down and scooped a handful of soil. "You want the most profitable thing on this farm? This is what they have that's valuable! It will be valuable not just today, or next week when you buy your next guitar. Year after year, it will keep producing something. When Kyan is a man, it will still be producing, and his sons after that. An idiot like you can never understand." I kicked his car door. "What is wrong with me? Why have I put up with you all this time?"

Edgar got out of the car and came charging at me. I didn't move. "What the hell? You dented my door! You know what this car means to me! Where's your head, Gigi?"

He came so close I could feel his breath on my face. I took the dirt in my hand and threw it at him. "I can't believe it's taken me this long to... I was so stupid! You almost ruined my life, Edgar Pepper! You're nothing and my son is so lucky you won't be there to damage him too! You need to leave!" I drew back to punch him with my dirty hand.

Edgar shielded his face. "Okay, okay! I'll go!" He backed away until he reached his car door. "This doesn't mean you're off the hook. I meant what I said: you've got two days to—"

My face and body were twisted in a combination of pain and realization, of the months I'd wasted on Edgar and his dreams. Pushing Kenneth away so Edgar could have whatever piece of me he wanted. He sucked the life out of me even when he wasn't there. I remembered the one last card in my hand to play.

"The only thing of value is below me."

"I'm not going to farm, Gigi. How many times is it gonna take to get it through your dumb head? I told you, I'm going to San Francisco. While you're here playing house with Kenny boy." He chuckled at the idea. "You make him noodles every night?"

I ignored his comment. Nothing he said mattered anymore. "Under us. The only thing of value is underneath where we're standing. See that?" I pointed to the vent just a few feet away. "There's a vent on top of the hill because there is a potato cellar underneath us."

Edgar threw his head back. "Oh, man." When he saw the serious look on my face, he bent over and sat on the ground, "Potatoes? You think I'm going to load up potatoes and make money on what? Tater chips? Oh, man. You poor girl."

I stormed toward him, kicking his leg as hard as I could. It felt good. I drew back to kick him again and he grabbed my legs. "Good thing I found out what kind of crazy you are now. This crap would distract me from my music."

"Not the potatoes, you fool. There's moonshine and a big still. It's been in there for decades. I guess it's all I have to give you." I squirmed away from him and moved to the vent. "Down here."

Edgar limped over to where I was standing. He didn't seem to feel pain. "What? You've got a still and you didn't tell me? Show me!"

"Only if you promise you're not ever coming back. Load up what you need and leave for good. Don't ever talk to Kenneth or his folks. And you're never going to see my son, like you would care. Have a nice life in San Francisco."

"Yeah, that's cool." Edgar limped to his car. "Tell me where it is and I'll pack up everything I can and be gone. I'm never coming back; you don't have to worry about that."

I walked over to the edge of Spud Hill and pointed downward. "Last time I checked, the padlock on the door is missing. Just drive inside so no one sees you and shut the door when you're done. And Edgar?"

"Huh?"

"His name is Kyan Brownwell. He's a great kid."

I drove back toward the house, feeling like a real person. Not the Georgina from last year, but someone better. For so many months I lived in a haze—scared and alone. But what I realized on my drive is that I had been just as alone with Edgar.

I paused by the main gate, where Kenneth was on a tractor with his yellow Pepper Implement-Ville cap pulled low over his eyes. I waved. He waved back and grinned widely. He was a good man. The best husband I could ask for.

After I put the motorcycle back in the barn, I found Frannie's strawberry bag and walked over to the Purple Wonder berries. I pulled back the protective netting placed to keep the birds away to expose an entire section of ripe berries. I gently removed them from the stems. The berries I pulled were plump and juicy. I put one in my mouth, the sweetest most perfect tasting berry I ever ate. The few Franniebell berries were over-ripe and falling off the stems, but I left them alone.

When I finished, I took the heavy bag into the kitchen and set them on the counter. Katherine was preparing a large chicken for the oven and nodded approvingly. "Looks like we'll have enough for jam. That will lift Francine's spirits."

I panicked. Did Frannie know something? Was that why she had been avoiding conversation lately? "Is she okay?"

"Oh, just tired. You know how busy things have been. Put your berries in the refrigerator. We don't rinse the dirt off until right before we eat them. Do you want to help me with these beautiful carrots from the garden?"

After the berries were safely stored away, I took a knife from the drawer and began quartering the multi-colored carrots, something I never knew existed until I moved to the farm. "Try one," Katherine encouraged.

I popped one in my mouth and experienced a sweet-ness almost equivalent to the strawberry I tried earlier.

"Wonderful, isn't it? Francine likes to pickle these. We'll help her with that in a couple of days. When you're in charge of the house, you'll want to keep your cellar full. You've seen all the jars of canned goods in the root cellar?"

I'd been in the root cellar numerous times, retrieving all manner of canned goods for dinner. It was almost as big as the Shoppe and Walke canned food section. I understood why Frannie was reluctant to buy those things when she went into town.

That night, after dinner, I knocked on Kenneth's door. "Can I come in?"

Kenneth answered the door in his pajamas, bleary-eyed. "I'm kinda tired tonight, Gigi. Do you need another book? You can just look through them." He opened the door wider and motioned for me to come in.

I sat down on his bed. "Kenneth, will you sit with me for a minute?"

He sat obediently by my side. I noticed how full his lips were, similar to Katherine's. He had a strong jaw, like his father's. His acne cleared and his face looked *handsome.* I gently stroked his cheek.

"I just wanted to say that I'm sorry. I don't know where my head has been. You've been here for me, not just now but all through high school. Nobody else did that. I've had the perfect man in front of me all this time and I couldn't see it."

His eyes opened wide. "Well, sure, Gigi. You know how much you mean to me, and I—"

"Shhh." I put my finger on his lips. "You are my husband." I laid back on the bed and pulled him on top of me. I took his face in my hands and gently kissed him. I unbuttoned his pajamas and touched his muscular chest, making little circles until I reached his flat stomach.

He grabbed my hand. "Are you sure?" he asked.

I nodded. I wanted to rid myself of Edgar more than I wanted to be with Kenneth at that moment. But something had changed in me.

As I sat, drinking my coffee the next morning, Frannie came into the kitchen and handed Kyan to me. He just finished a bath and smelled like baby powder and freshly washed clothing. "I'll be back soon. Can you watch him?"

I pressed his sweet face to my lips. "Hi, son." I hugged him tightly for a few minutes, rocking back and forth as I had seen Frannie do hundreds of times. His normally squirmy body became still. When I allowed the feelings to come, it seemed right. Kyan felt like my baby.

I could hear Frannie and Katherine in the formal dining room. "Something has changed," Frannie said in a low voice.

"The girl has certainly gained confidence. I attribute it to my tutelage," Katherine replied, not caring to lower her voice. "And of course your cooking, Francine."

The three of us worked late into the next afternoon, chopping the juicy berries. "My secret to the best jam is to use freshly-picked produce. Berries have to be used within a day. And this," Frannie produced a large lemon from the back of the counter, "is my secret weapon. I have a lemon tree on the other side of the barn. Harlan made me a nice hothouse for it years ago. I don't tell anyone because I'm the only person in the entire county with a lemon tree. They would think I was a little uppity."

"Francine, don't leave the girl thinking you've given her the entire recipe to the best jam in the county." Katherine itched her nose with the crook of her elbow. "Your mother-in-law doesn't share that recipe with anyone. We'll have to leave in a bit so she can add her ingredients alone. It's like she's got the recipe for world peace. Nonsense if you ask me."

"The day will come," Frannie said, staring out the kitchen window.

Chapter 22

Kenneth

"IT DON'T SEEM right, you stayin' home." Dad looked at Mom with concern. "Don't you want to take your picture next to your first-prize ribbon and jam?"

Mom smiled. She'd recently taken to sitting in her robe, bouncing Kyan on her lap while she drank her coffee. Today she hadn't even taken the sponge rollers out. "How long has it been since I've had the place to myself? I love my family, but I need to spend some time just breathing."

Dad stood and pushed his chair in. "You sayin' you can't breathe around your family? Doesn't sound like you, Frannie."

"Dad, Mom just means she wants some time to herself. With her grandson and company—no offense, Aunt Katherine—and new family, she's probably just tired." I took a plate of scrambled eggs to my seat, pausing to ruffle my son's hair. Kyan gurgled happily and kicked his legs.

Katherine sat up straight in her chair and looked at Mom. "Your mother deserves to be alone. You and Georgina can handle the baby, I assume? It will be your first time alone with him. I'll enjoy viewing the subpar canned entries and watching the awkward young people fumble around the fairgrounds with their offspring. No offense, Kenneth."

I smiled. As a young child, I'd been afraid of her. She always wore a stern look on her face and didn't move to the side when I came barreling through the room. Running into Katherine meant a toy in the eye, or worse, a hand to the brow. "Stop! Rabbits run. Children skip in a controlled manner. Next time you'll remember."

Even though she seemed cold and unfeeling, she sent large presents every birthday and Christmas. She wrote cards of encouragement when I won the spelling bee and the Math Whiz Quiz. Her visits were usually brief and to the point, so it seemed odd she extended her stay this time for several weeks.

My beautiful wife, dressed in bell-bottom jeans and a pretty pink blouse Mom bought for her, poured herself a cup of coffee. I couldn't believe it; she had experienced some kind of awakening, deciding she wanted to be with me and our son. Mom told me the day would come, just to be patient.

She's never been wrong.

"Morning, all." Gigi bent down and kissed Kyan's cheek and squeezed my shoulder. I caught her hand and held it tightly. I blushed thinking about our second night together. I was secretly glad Gigi had some experience with men. Well, with Edgar.

She knew things that were probably in those books Mom gave me but made me squeamish to read. It left me with more questions than answers. I hesitated to tell her about our current situation. Usually, she figured things out on her own, but she seemed distracted lately. Maybe soon we would surprise her with another grandchild.

Later, as we loaded the car for our day, Mom scurried about, making sure we included everything she felt necessary. "You have the diaper bag? I put enough diapers in for two days. And extra clothes. You know how he can surprise you. The fancy folding stroller is in the trunk. Do you know how to unfold it?"

"You showed us five times, Mom. Gigi's got the baby food jars and the milk. We've got the ice chest packed to keep things cool. We'll do fine." I patted her on the back. "Don't worry. We'll take good care of your grandson."

I sat down in the car beside Georgina and put my arms out. "Give him to me, please."

"I'd feel better if you put him in that car seat." She put a protective hand over Kyan's head.

Dad started the engine and leaned forward to look at his wife. "Never had one of those contraptions for Kenneth. He did just fine. Hand the baby to the boy. We need to get on the road."

Katherine braided her long, dark hair and swirled it on top of her head; she even wore a touch of dark, red lipstick. She looked about as nice as I'd ever seen her look. She opened the back door and pushed her massive, striped purse into the seat before heaving herself into the car. "Don't worry, Francine. We'll all be fine, although you'll be missing the entertainment that is misbehaved wildlings running and eating unattended until they vomit unspecified colors all over the carnival rides. I'll be happy to update you upon our return. You just enjoy your day."

Mom handed her grandson to me and shut the door.

I held my wife's hand all the way to town, watching her hair blow in the wind from the open window. Every now and again she looked over at me and smiled.

When we passed through the SPRITZ COUNTY WELCOMES YOU arch, Dad had to circle the dirt parking lot four times before a space opened up. The seafoam green Cadillac (the one Mom called the "Sunday car" because of its rare usage) barely fit in the narrow space between haphazardly parked pickups. Dad suggested I help Aunt Katherine squeeze out of the narrow space between the car door and the neighboring vehicle, causing her to snap, "The day hasn't yet come when I need the help of any man to stand on my own two feet."

The fairgrounds consisted of a series of long, white buildings and carnival rides shaded from the late summer sun by tall oak trees. One building held all the exhibits created by people in the community, including school children and adults who showed off their baked goods and sewing projects. Another contained livestock primped for the show ring. The third building housed the eating area, with long rows of picnic tables in the middle and stations for hot food, pie, and ice cream lining the walls.

By the time we reached the fairgrounds, Kyan was asleep on my shoulder. I slid out of the car and carefully handed Kyan to Georgina while I unloaded the trunk.

"We'll plan to meet back here at four. That should give me time to look at the livestock and you all to do your people watchin'. That work, son?"

"Sure, Dad." After several attempts, I finally unfolded the stroller and Kyan was resting comfortably, still asleep. "Did Mom pack us a picnic? That's what we always do at the fair, Gigi."

"Your mother has far too much to worry about this summer to concern herself with picnics," Aunt Katherine remarked curtly. "There is an establishment on the grounds for meals. My recollection is that they also serve pies. Not as good what I would make, mind you. But sufficient."

"Four, then. Take good care of the boy. Your mother would be a mess if we came home with a hair out of place on the grandson."

I pushed the stroller over the uneven gravel until we reached the cement walkway. "I remember seeing you here last year, Gigi. You came with Edgar. He was staring at other girls. You didn't look happy."

Georgina's happy face turned sullen. I regretted bringing him up.

"He was looking at other girls? I never knew that. We'd just started dating. It seemed like he was madly in love with me." She looked like she wanted to say more, but she was silent.

Quickly, I changed the subject. "One year, I begged Mom to let me show some livestock. She bought me a calf and helped me wash and feed Darcy–a name I chose from a Jane Austen book Mom and I were reading together. When the time came to show her, I came to the realization she would be sold for slaughter when we finished and I couldn't go through with it. Dad sold her privately to Thrasher Farm under the condition they would never slaughter her. Somehow, she disappeared one summer. Never explained to me what happened."

"I'm sorry, Kenneth."

She grabbed my arm and pulled me close. I wondered if other married people experienced that electricity every time their partner was close? I would have to ask Mom.

"Do you want to go look at the schoolwork?" Georgina asked. Teachers from Pepperville Elementary would choose the best artwork from their students to display at the fair. The top students in each grade received a ribbon and a 50-cent coupon to the Cluck Hut.

We entered the first, long building and began looking at the colorful drawings and creations. "Gigi? Is that you?" The voice, so childish and endearing, belonged to her brother.

"Calvin!" She bent down and scooped him up in her arms. "I've missed you so much. You smell like breakfast cereal and dirt. I've missed that too!"

"We have to go to Mrs. Logan's house after school now. She's mean. We can only have one snack and she hits us on the head when we don't behave." He pulled his dirty t-shirt to his face, where he used it to wipe his nose.

"I'm sorry. That can't be fun." Georgina looked at me somberly. I nodded.

"Calvin, this is Kenneth. He's my husband."

"Your husband? You're an old lady then? I thought you went to college or something." Calvin eyed me suspiciously. "Are you old, too?"

I bent down and stuck my hand out. "No sirree. Just startin' life. I'm pleased to meet you, though." Calvin hesitated and then shook my hand heartily, yanking until I stood up.

Kyan began to stir, making gurgling noises. "Is that your kid?"

"This is Kyan. He's your nephew. Isn't that cool?"

Calvin scrunched up his face, clearly confused. "He's your kid? He doesn't look like you."

Georgina sighed. "Babies just look like babies. He'll look like me when he grows up."

"You guys ran off! I've been looking for a good fifteen minutes!"

My body tightened. I squeezed Gigi's arm. "Hiya, Lois. Long time no see."

Lois looked at my face and then at Gigi's. "I never thought I'd run into you."

"Are you with my brothers?" Gigi asked, unable to disguise the hurt in her voice.

"Yeah... um... your mom had some kind of meeting

Joann Keder

at work and your dad has the flu. They wanted the boys
to see the fair and..."

"It's hard to believe they'd talk to you after I was
gone. I didn't realize you had that kind of relationship."
Gigi's voice was shaky.

"It's weird you'd be here with her brothers; kinda
seems like you've formed some kind of alliance, the
three of you," I added.

"I'm not strong like you." Lois's eyes got red and
tears began to flow. Then Gigi started crying as well.
Mom said lots of girls cried in pairs. "My mom lost her
job last month. She got fired for... She stole some
money from Flowers, Flowers, and Fudge. So, I called
your parents and asked if I could babysit every now and
then to make some extra money. That's all it is."

Georgina took a deep breath and let it out slowly.
"Really, I need to thank you, Lois. If it wasn't for your
'experience' with Edgar, Kenneth and I wouldn't have
ended up together." She stuck her hand out. "Thank
you."

Lois shook her hand, trying to come in closer for a
hug, but Gigi kept her arms stiff.

"Can we go now?" Calvin asked. "I'm getting bored."

"Sure, Brett," Lois said as she bent down to look at
Kyan. "He sure is cute. Looks just like you, Kenneth."

"You should probably find Brett—the real one."

Gigi smiled. "Great seeing you."

When they were gone, I rubbed Gigi's shoulders. "That
took a lot of courage. I'm sure it wasn't easy."

194

She put her head on my shoulder. "Not as hard as you'd think. I've figured out who I need in my life. But seeing my brother was hard. My parents didn't even tell the boys. Even after they planned out my life with Edgar's parents."

"I know," I said quietly.

We walked to the next barn over, where they were serving sloppy Joes and potato chips. When we found our seats and fed Kyan his lunch, I pushed my plate away and looked at Georgina. "Gigi, I gotta tell you something."

"Okay... I'll do the next diaper change, I promise." She laughed.

"No, it's about Edgar's parents. I haven't told you anything because you haven't been yourself for a while. So, I...well, you know my folks, especially my mom–they like to be in control. They had to take care of some stuff for us."

"What kind of stuff?" She eyed me warily.

"My dad will be needin' a new tractor next year, what with the extra land we acquired and the new hired hands. Pepper Implement-Ville is the only place in town. So, Dad had to go out there and find a way to work with Edgar's dad."

"What did he do?" She was starting to look panicked.

"He told Edgar's dad that you weren't sure about the baby's daddy. That Edgar might not be the one. Mr. Pepper called you a bunch of names, and Dad said if he wanted Brownwell business he'd never talk like that again. Then he told him everything I've shared with Mom about Edgar for the past four years. Mr.

Pepper was so upset he fired his son right then and there."

"So, Edgar got fired because of me? That's terrible. I'm... I feel like I'm going to be sick. Can you take Kyan?" She got up and covered her mouth.

"Not you, Gigi. Edgar. He caused all of these problems!" I called after her.

When she returned a few minutes later, her face was relaxed. I was tickling Kyan's hands, loving the sound of a baby dissolving in giggles.

"I'm sorry about that. Today has been a lot to handle. Can we walk around a little more? We should go see your mom's strawberry jam."

We walked in silence through the rest of the buildings, until we reached the one filled with the largest produce in the county and all the preserves. A 50-pound watermelon and a nearly 100-pound yellow squash took the top honors. Mom's watermelon pickles took home the top prize, as usual.

On a shelf in the back of the building, the jams and jellies were displayed. When we reached that area, we stared in shock at the top shelf, reserved for the grand prize winner. Martha Prembone's Berries Berserk garnered the large grand-prize ribbon. Mom's Jammin' Purple Wonder was delegated to second place.

"Well, this day is sure full of surprises." I didn't want to think about the look on Mom's face. I hated when she was disappointed.

Gigi gasped. "Oh no! Your mom will be devastated! There must be a mistake!"

I could see Gigi was getting upset again. I didn't want either one of the women in my life hurting. "I think Mom'll understand. Somebody else needs a chance every now and then. She always told me number one is temporary. Builds character to be the underdog next year." I glanced at the oversized clock above the giant squash section. "We should probably head back to the car."

"Kenneth, there's something I should tell you about Edgar."

"Well, he's gone to San Francisco now. That's what Dad said. He won't be botherin' us anymore. While we were working on machine repair in the barn, Dad says to me, 'You don't need to worry, son. Your mother reports he's left town.' Sometimes I don't mind she's so damn nosy."

Gigi shook her head. "No, he isn't. At least the last I heard he wasn't. He's been blackmailing me."

She told me the whole story, right there in front of Mom's second-place jam. That she almost slept with Edgar on our farm. I knew she was still under his spell, but I didn't realize how much. I had a rotten feeling in my gut. It must've been how she felt when she saw Lois.

"Gosh darn, Gigi." I banged my hand on the stroller, causing Kyan to look away from the rambunctious kids he was studying across the room momentarily. "I wish you would've told me. We could have taken care of this sooner. If his dad knew he was still lurkin' around... Why didn't you say anything?"

"Because I thought I loved Edgar. I thought he was taking me with him. I thought we were going to make a life together. I was wrong about all those things. It turns out I already had one right here."

It took me a minute to process. Then I realized what she was saying. That she chose me over him. I hugged her tightly. I tried kissing her on the cheek, but she grabbed my face and kissed me on the lips.

Kyan slept again on the way home while we held hands. Georgina put her head on my shoulder. Aunt Katherine told us in detail about the inferior stitching on the quilts were like "nothing she experienced in all her years of quilt gazing."

As we came around the last corner before the farm, a large cloud of black smoke came into view.

"What's that, Dad?" I wondered for a minute if we had done something careless.

Dad was silent until we got closer. "Something on our place went up in smoke."

Chapter 23

Frannie

I TURNED AWAY quickly from the car so they wouldn't see my tears. I knew it was time to let Kyan start bonding with his parents, but that didn't make it easy. It would feel good to have some time alone though.

After pulling out my curlers and brushing my hair, I looked at the mirror with satisfaction. I was almost sixty and barely had a grey hair to show for it. My years on the big farm had been good ones, and as Katherine reminded me, "Living a good life is all the youthful potion one needs."

I brewed a pot of lemon and lavender tea and brought the teapot and my cup to the front porch, where I was able to sit and rock for the first time all summer. Having a baby brought new life to the farm and to me, but there were other things in life that were almost as enjoyable, and I had neglected them.

As I rocked, I watched the barn cats chasing one of the skittish dogs around the yard. A litter of kittens born in the spring were old enough to feel courageous in their pursuit of the dog as well. That was, until their mother intervened and guided them away. "A mother's job is never done," I said.

Something clicked in my head at that moment. I set my tea down and walked out to the barn, where I picked up a can of gas and some matches. I put the gas in the back of the pickup and drove over to the other side of the farm, to the top of Spud Hill. I took the can of gasoline out of the pickup and began to pour it into the vent.

I was surprised to hear a clinking sound. I put the gas can down and listened again. It was louder and more pronounced. I opened the back of the pickup, looking for something to take with me, and found only a shovel.

Carefully, I crept down the hill and to the doors of the cellar, which were uncharacteristically wide open. I would have to talk to Kenneth about leaving things unsecured. Last year, he left the barn doors open and several wild turkeys flew in, leaving a mess of feces and feathers in their wake.

When I walked inside and my eyes adjusted to the darkness, I saw a familiar vehicle parked toward the back, next to the still. Edgar was loading bottles of potato vodka into boxes and placing them in the trunk of his car.

"What are you doing here?"

He looked up, startled. "Gigi... Georgina told me I could take this. I sold some last week and made 200 bucks. I need the money so I can leave town."

I eyed him suspiciously. "You shouldn't be here. You're trespassing,"

"No, I told you, it's cool. I'm just getting a few more. Then I'll leave."

"I think you should leave now. That's not your property."

Edgar put the box down and smiled a sleazy smile he'd no doubt used to woo many doe-eyed teenage girls.

"You probably don't know this, but that kid—he's mine. Gigi and I, we made him. Can't imagine Gigi sleeping with Ken. No offense."

I didn't give him the satisfaction of a reaction. I inched slightly closer to him, raising my shovel in case I needed to protect myself.

"You probably don't want me spreading it around. If people in this town knew your grandson was really someone else's, well, I can imagine it'd be real embarrassing."

"I guess you'd imagine wrong." I smiled. "And, just out of curiosity, what are you proposing—that perhaps you would leave town, never to return in exchange for something from me?"

Edgar pointed his finger at me. "Now you're a smart lady. I didn't think Ken would have come from someone like that. No offense. He's kind of... simple."

"How much? What's the number?"

Edgar looked up, pretending to calculate living expenses. In truth, I doubt he had any idea how much it would take. His daddy paid for everything. "Oh, probably a thousand. But I'd need cash. My dad closed my account. Don't want to get too greedy."

"I probably have that much cash in the safe at home. You'll have to wait here while I get it. I don't want anyone seeing you."

"No problem. I can hang out here for a while. There's plenty to quench my thirst." He bent down and picked up a bottle.

I went back to the house, mostly to gather my wits. There would be no going back from this. I paused to glance at the family picture we took after Kenneth's eighth-grade graduation. Kenneth and Harlan were wearing matching blue-checkered shirts and tall cowboy hats. The photographer asked them to remove their hats, but Kenneth insisted they wear them, he and his dad. We were all smiling brightly that day, holding hands as the photographer counted down, *three... two... one...*

I returned to the potato cellar with Gigi's strawberry-picking bag.

Edgar stood up, wobbling. "This shit is strong." He put his hand out, grasping at an imaginary bar.

"Before you go, you need to know two things."

"Don't you want to get rid of me? Or maybe you've got a thing for me. Wouldn't be the first old lady. I could tell you stories..."

"Do you want the money or not?"

Edgar sighed. "Get on with it."

"First, I know everything that happens in this town. EVERYTHING. I've spent my entire life keeping my eyes open to protect the ones I love. You haven't made one pathetic move that I didn't know about ten minutes after it happened. Every time you dropped your drawers... Don't go thinking, Mr. Edgar Pepper, that you're the smart one here. And second, there is nothing I wouldn't do for my son or grandson. Nothing."

"Whatever. You wanna claim my kid? Go ahead. Give me the money and I'll get out of your cellar."

I stared at him. This drunk, ignorant man who had caused my son and my daughter-in-law so much turmoil. Everything in my life had been for Kenneth or Harlan. Each piece of information intercepted; every bribe paid; each time I knew in my mind I was protecting my family from some potential threat. This time it was for Kyan.

I reached out to the side with my hand holding the heavy bag and swung it around hard, hitting him in the head. The garden stones Katherine so carefully painted to line the strawberry patch, one for each year she came to visit, hit Edgar on the side of his head and knocked him on the ground. I moved to his side and looked at him for a moment before I raised the bag over my head and hit him again.

I left the cellar, shut the door, and walked up to the top of the hill, to the vent. I lit a match and dropped it inside. I wasn't in any particular hurry to get back to my truck, knowing the vodka wasn't close to where the vent was located. By the time the entire cellar blew, I was on the road to the other side of the farm.

I took a long bubble bath, feeling more peace than I had in days. Afterward, I headed to the kitchen to grind up the leftover ham from lunch two days ago to use for ham salad sandwiches for dinner. It was what I would have normally brought to the fair, and I didn't want my family to miss out on that experience. I put five olive-colored placemats on the table, filled five glasses with sun tea, and then sat on the porch, patiently waiting for my family's return.

The car was barely in park when Kenneth hopped out and ran up to me. "What's goin' on?"

Harlan jumped out and came up the steps. "You decide to roast some marshmallows without us, Frannie?"

I crossed my arms. "I told you boys to get rid of that cellar. Over and over. Decided if no one else was worried about keeping my grandson safe, I'd have to do it myself."

Kenneth shaded his eyes and stared at the ominous black smoke. "You sure it's taken care of? Shouldn't I go out and push some dirt on top of it, make sure it's not going to start anything else on fire?"

"No, it's fine, son." Harlan took his cap off and opened the screen door. "Probably collapsed on itself by now. You can take the dozer out tomorrow and fill it with dirt. That'll keep it from sparkin'. I can spare you for an hour or two."

Georgina walked up to the porch with Kyan. She handed him to me, and I immediately pulled him close and kissed his face all over. Georgina studied me as I loved on my grandson. She had been worried the first day we burned our trash. The clouds of black smoke were a part of life on the farm.

"It's my project," I said firmly. "I'll fill it in. It's no different than when we burn the garbage. I'll be up before you boys and get it taken care of. There'll be no more talk of potato cellars."

Georgina's body tensed, her eyes widening. "You

burned the cellar? Will all of that vodka inside? Wasn't it valuable?"

I smiled. "Nothing for you to worry about. Who's ready for ham salad and corn casserole?"

Georgina ran off, upset. I started to tell Kenneth to go after her, but he was already halfway down the steps. By the time they returned, we were almost finished eating dinner. I tried not to show them how much it upset me that they would miss out on my ham salad.

"The stitching, Francine. You should have seen the shoddy work. How these people can show their faces at the county fair is beyond me. I saw them giggling and carrying on like they'd just quilted the Sistine Chapel. Why not just *paste* the fabric together?" Katherine rambled on and on about the fair until our plates were empty. Harlan stood up.

"Wait a minute. I have something I have to tell everyone. Could you please sit?" Georgina looked at Kenneth. He nodded and took her hand.

"I've done some things wrong. Lots of things. I guess I was just naïve in thinking... I'm sorry. I didn't mean to hurt anyone—"

"Life is too short for these conversations." I felt panicked. Things were falling out of my control and I didn't like it.

"Let the girl talk, dear," Harlan insisted.

"I'm dying," I blurted.

Chapter 24

Katherine

A S A GIRL, I was often laughed at for my elongated, "horse-shaped" face and jutting chin. "Put a bit in her mouth," the boys in my class chided. "Give her an apple when she whinnies," the pretty girls would say, giggling as they circled me on the playground. I didn't care. In fact, some days I pulled my shiny, sable hair back tightly so it hung down my back like a horsetail. If they were going to call me names, I would play the part.

Being the oldest of four children, I always felt it was my duty to show the others how to behave. At age fourteen, I was already acting as a parent to my two younger sisters and younger brother while my parents worked hard hoeing weeds and harvesting crops for neighbors as sharecroppers. I made toys out of dried corncobs and empty Lima bean cans.

To my parents' credit, they felt strongly that I continue my studies past the eighth grade and graduate from high school. The Depression hit Pepperville hard, but no one felt it more than the children who gave up a bright future to drop out of school and work alongside their parents. I did my homework while bouncing baby Harlan on my knee. I made supper if there was any to be had and bathed all the children before putting them to bed.

When my parents and two sisters developed high fevers, I stayed home from school to care for them. One of the neighbors kindly took Harlan so I could concentrate my efforts on my parents and sisters. I stood outside each night and allowed myself ten minutes to cry while my parents clutched their abdomens and writhed in pain.

The doctor, who had been distracted by an unusually high number of births that year, finally made a visit to our unpainted shanty. His diagnosis wasn't encouraging. My parents and sisters had contracted typhoid fever, something increasingly rare in the country. As near as he could tell, a drifter who worked three days during harvest brought the disease. My father was charged with firing him when he complained of a headache and didn't work for three days. The hapless fellow left the town of Pepperville, never to be seen again.

The doctor also informed us that any one of our family members may not survive the illness. He warned me that if they were to become delirious, the end was near. I was determined to see them through.

At the tender age of fourteen, I had seen the family exist on a single bag of flour for a week.

My mother became too weak to move. My sisters' cries eventually stopped. One night, my father rose in the middle of the night, dressed, and calmly asked me to help him saddle the horse.

"We sold the horse two years ago, Papa."

I was pleased he seemed better. I stood in the doorway, watching him as he went into the yard.

"I'm going to town for milk then," he said with a smile. "Tell your mother I'll be back in a few hours." He put his hand on his head and walked out the door, collapsing on top of the chicken coop. When I tried in vain to move him, I realized he had been impaled on the nails that came loose while no one was available to make repairs.

My mother passed the next morning. Years later, I confessed to Harlan that I may have given up caring for my sisters at that point. I knew the inevitable.

The neighbors came and helped me get back on my feet. The chicken coop was repaired, the house was cleaned. The two-bedroom home now seemed overly spacious. And also quite lonely.

I insisted that Harlan be returned to my care. A kind neighbor said Harlan and I could live with her elderly mother in town. The woman would care for Harlan while I went to school, and I would cook and clean in return.

Later, I agreed to leave Harlan there for the year it would take me to complete teacher's college. He was thriving as a young boy, devoid of the memories of death that plagued me. When I returned with my teaching degree, I rented a small place in town so that he could go to the grade school where I taught.

Harlan grew into a lanky boy with a broad forehead and square jaw, avoiding the jeers I'd faced. He was happy and upbeat, despite being an orphan. At the age of sixteen, he decided to quit school and become a sharecropper just as his father had done. He harbored dreams of becoming a wealthy farmer, something I found absurd. "You're a Brownwell. We're hardworking and proud. But we aren't wealthy."

It was hard to escape the guilt I felt for surviving past the age of my parents. I didn't allow myself to enjoy life or engage in any sort of relationship beyond the courteous discourse required between myself and other staff members. It wouldn't have been right.

I was finally free to pursue life somewhere else. Within a year, I quit my job and left for Moline, Illinois where I could sit beside the Mississippi and listen to the water lapping at the shore while I read books about exotic cultures and made-up worlds.

My hair began to grey, a reminder of old age I detested. I wound it tightly on my head and covered it with a scarf. I didn't speak to anyone as they walked by while I sat on the wooden bench reading a book and gazing occasionally at the river. Certainly, I looked like a bitter old woman who had given up on life and friendship.

"I see you're reading Hemingway."

I looked up to see a handsome gentleman with aquamarine eyes and full lips staring at me. I pulled my coat tighter around my body.

"He seems a rather sullen chap, don't you agree?"

Joann Keder

"Sir, I'm not here for conversation. I spend my week-days in the company of thirty-five teens. I don't wish to engage in more inane repartee." I closed my book and bent down to place it in my large, brown purse.

"You're a teacher? What grade? I teach fourth grade students. Love their enthusiasm."

I paused, trying to determine if this merited a full discussion. I hadn't called Harlan this week, so I decided this could count as my socialization.

"I teach literature. To high school students. I have no tolerance for the young ones. Until they can think and act like real people, I'm not interested in their silly banter."

He threw his head back and laughed. It caused me to experience unexpected emotions. "Why do you find that funny?"

"You're not fond of children? In your profession? Not married, I take it."

I frowned. "Very forward of you, sir,"

"I'm so sorry. That wasn't my intent. I'm new to the city, here from Chicago. I just hunger for someone to converse with on the weekends. Callahan Blackburn." He offered his hand to me and I stared at it warily.

"Callahan—very strange. Is it a family name?"

"Yes. Generations of strangely-named gentlemen. I'm actually the fourth."

I took his hand and shook it briefly before pulling back into the safety of my space. "What brings you to Moline?"

210

"I needed a change of pace. My fiancé and I... it didn't end well. I wanted to try life from a different angle for a bit. And you?"

I pursed my lips. I hadn't told anyone of my life in Pepperville. "Pursuing a different angle as well."

"If you'll allow me, I would love to exchange books with you. I have several at home that might interest you. They are collecting dust more than anything, and I'd love to share them with a fellow bibliophile."

I abandoned all reason and nodded. The following weekend, he returned with a copy of *Titus Alone*. Slowly, I began to anticipate and actually enjoy conversations with him. It felt good, having someone interested in the minutiae of my life.

"My poor brother and his wife. They've been trying for years to have a baby. Francine has been cursed with many dead children. Though I have no tolerance for them, I can imagine the extreme anguish they must be experiencing."

Callahan nodded. "I've had some family issues myself. I'll be returning to Chicago for a few weeks. My father is ill and I need to make sure his affairs are in order."

I put my arm on his. "Oh, I'm so sorry! You must be beside yourself." When I realized I touched him, I pulled my arm away. He looked down and smiled, gently placing my arm back on his.

"He is a difficult man. I've both anticipated and dreaded what would happen when he passed. I appreciate your concern."

I blushed, feeling like I had become too familiar. I

was a middle-aged woman, and carrying on like this seemed rather silly. But I did enjoy his company.

"Since I'm going to be away for a bit, I'm wondering if you might like to go to my apartment and find some books to tide you over. Call it a 'specialized library'."

I'd been in his acquaintance for several months. He seemed kind and caring, and a short visit to his apartment would be appropriate. "Yes, Callahan. I'd enjoy that."

It wasn't surprising to see he lived in a fancy part of town. Nor was I especially surprised when he showed me the three bedrooms and formal dining area in his "apartment". What did surprise me was that he had accumulated thousands of books.

"This must've taken your entire life!" I marveled at the floor-to-ceiling collection. The pristine copy of Kurt Vonnegut's *The Sirens of Titan* caught my eye.

"These are alphabetized, just like the library, so if you aren't taking it, please replace it accordingly," he cautioned. "Would you like a drink?"

"I don't drink. But I would enjoy some water."

Callahan laughed a deep, throaty laugh that I had come to find comforting. "Oh, my dear Katherine. You need to live a bit. Why don't I make you a martini? Just so that you know what they are when you read about them?"

I hesitated for a moment. "Okay. Just one."

I sipped on the pleasurable yet bitter-tasting drink as I browsed his bookshelf. "I think this is giving me a headache."

"Please sit."

I sat on his couch and held my head. "Oh, my. I don't believe I've experienced this before. I hope it isn't typhoid..."

He laughed again. "My dear. You are a treat." He took my hand and gently massaged it. "I read a book on the great healing powers of touch. The hands, especially, benefit from a robust massage."

I stared at him, feeling warm and loving emotions that didn't exist in me until I'd made his acquaintance. Harlan was the only man allowed this much intimacy in my world, until now.

"I wonder if I could be so bold as to ask if you would want to... date me. I know that I'm old and you're young and handsome but..."

Callahan pulled me close and kissed me passionately. I didn't resist.

"I'm not looking for a young woman with no experience. Those types bore me. I want a woman on my arm who knows things about the world. I can think of no one else to better represent the type."

Though I later had no idea how I allowed things to progress so far, this man whose beauty and charm surpassed any others I'd encountered took me to his bedroom. He showed me things previously existing only on the pages of my novels, the steamy pages I was unable to skip due to plot progression. The next morning, he kissed me sweetly and told me he would call when he returned from Chicago.

I returned every week to our meeting spot on the bench. Despite the fact that he said he would be gone for a while, I kept hoping my allure would be so strong that he couldn't stay away. I wrote him letters every day, though I hadn't a clue where to send them. I even took the bus over to his apartment and stood outside waiting. I was angry at my gullibility. Strong, survivor Katherine never let a man get in the way of regular living.

Finally, one blustery day as I sat on the bench watching the angry river bubbling and churning, I smelled the familiar scent of his expensive cologne. "Callahan! I thought you'd left for good!"

He bent down and kissed my cheek. "No, things turned out to be more complicated than I anticipated. Do you want to get out of this weather? You could pick out more books."

I heartily agreed to all that entailed. I'd simply lost control of all sense of reason. That was the one thing I knew for sure. But my heart didn't care. My desire overtook my common sense.

We met every night for almost three weeks. I assumed, due to the normal development of story in all the books I'd read, that he would be proposing soon. I was staunchly against marriage. After thirty, it seemed inappropriate anyway. But Callahan was something—someone—I hadn't experienced before.

On the fourth night of the fourth week, everything changed. As I was lying in his arms stroking the dark hair on his chest, he began to fidget. "What is it, my love?" I asked.

"I need to tell you something. Because you're a mature, modern woman, I know you'll understand."

My heart sunk. I began experiencing flashbacks of my family, of being abandoned because of illness and death. "What is it?"

"I'm going to return to Chicago. My family needs me."

I sat up. "You're leaving? I would think they would have dealt with your father's death by now." The satin sheet slid away, revealing an imperfect body that normally hid in the dark. I had given up my last grasp on decency, allowing him to see me naked.

"No, it's not my father. I need to return to my wife. The reason—the real reason—I went back was to marry."

"But you broke up. You were done with her..."

"My family is influential. Though things were difficult, we found that for our families, we still needed to create a merger. That's what this is more about: business. But you, my love, you are my heart." He reached for my face, but I slapped his hand away.

"You want us to continue our relationship? While you're married?"

"I can return whenever we want to be together. I'm sure my wife will have side interests as well. It's not so complicated. That's how things are done in our circles."

I walked out of his life, but not before pulling as many books as I could into my overnight bag. I slammed his door so hard the expensive portrait he commissioned of himself riding a racehorse came crashing to the ground. I refused to allow myself to feel heartbroken. It was to be expected for letting my guard down.

What happened next made perfect sense.

Chapter 25

Georgina

"WHY DIDN'T YOU tell me afore now? Just blurtin' things out in front of the kids?"

Harlan stared hard at his wife. "Well, what is it? Are you gonna tell us what's goin' on or not?"

"It's cancer. I've been tired for a few months. Doctor Andrews says there isn't anything that can be done. It's too advanced." Frannie looked down at her half-eaten sandwich. "I figured I might as well just enjoy my family as long as I could, without having you all fuss over me. I think I won't have the energy for much before too long, so now seemed as good a time as any to make an announcement."

Kenneth left the table and stood in front of the sink. "This can't be right. Your doc is pretty old. He might not know the latest treatments. Can we go somewhere else? I've heard good things about the clinic in Stanswick."

I wanted to comfort him, but Frannie was at his side

in an instant. She hugged him from behind and then spun him around. She put her hands on either side of his face and pulled him close. "Oh, son. I don't want to deal with more white coats and worried looks. I just want to enjoy what's left. See my grandson every day and hope that he remembers my face."

"What kind is it? Do you know? Maybe I can go to the library and do some research. There has to be something." Kenneth bent down and hugged his mother. His face was ashen. "What can we do, Mom?"

"It's in my organs. It's my choice and I don't want to share any more than that. It doesn't really matter now."

I looked at my husband, tears streaming down his face. In a matter of minutes, I'd gone from worrying about being thrown out on the street for my deception to wondering how I might survive on the farm without my mother-in-law's guidance. Frannie was my lifeline, the caretaker for my son and the replacement mother I needed.

"Frannie... I can't... this is awful. Just awful." I ran up to my bedroom, not the one I was now sharing with Kenneth, but the one I used as a hiding place all the months I lived there. For the second time today, I was completely overwhelmed.

I put my face in the pillow so that no one would hear my sobs. I didn't deserve to feel as badly as the rest of the family, but the feeling of loss was overwhelming. After several minutes, there was a knock at the door.

"Who is it?" I wiped my face hard, trying to remove any evidence of emotion.

Katherine opened the door and, without thinking, I

ran to her and pressed my face into her large chest. "Why is this happening?" I sobbed.

"None of that now..." Katherine stroked my hair. "Don't let Francine hear you. She feels bad enough."

"I'm sorry. I just don't know what I'll do without her. She has taught me so much. And Kenneth will be devastated. And Kyan..."

"I'll tell you what you'll do. You'll decide to act like you're a real parent now. No more staying in bed until you wish. And you'll have to do her farm work. That's what she wants: to know her place is in good hands. All the gardening will be on your shoulders and I'll help you learn anything else. It will be hard, but we'll keep our chins up and see it through."

I pulled my head back, staring at the old woman's stern face. "Why aren't you upset? Doesn't it bother you at all?"

Katherine scowled. "Of course, child. Don't accuse me of being a cold fish. I've known about Francine's illness ever since I arrived. She asked me not to tell anyone until she was ready. I promised I would stay on as long as I was needed."

The next morning, I awoke before Kenneth. I went down and made coffee and eggs and then waited patiently for Frannie to come down with Kyan. To my surprise, my mother-in-law came in the back door looking disheveled.

"You made coffee! Thank you, hon. I took the back hoe out. Been out filling the old potato cellar with dirt. No more Spud Hill. But all chapters have an ending."

Tears filled my eyes, but I couldn't allow emotion to

overtake me today. I remembered Edgar and his threats. "Did you clean it out first? The still? Is it gone?"

Frannie smiled. "I found just the right place for the alcohol. An 'interested buyer', let's say. We'll have no more talk of that. Understood?"

"Was it Edgar? Did you know about—"

Frannie put her finger to her lips. "Shhh. Your worries are your husband and son. I'm sure Kyan is stirring. I'll go get him and you can make his oatmeal. You remember how I taught you?"

I wanted to know more, but I realized Frannie was tight-lipped. Even at this stage of her life, my mother-in-law wouldn't divulge more information than she felt necessary. "I'll start on his breakfast."

As the fall days became shorter, I tried my best to go into the garden each day. Frannie instructed me to pull the plants that were done producing and mulch the ground to protect the soil for winter. I kept the straw from blowing away with composted chicken manure from Harlan's chickens on top, being careful not to cover the root bases themselves with the manure so it wouldn't hinder their initial sprouting in the spring.

My anxiety over Edgar eventually subsided. Frannie must've sold him the alcohol or he would have returned. Sometimes I thought of him playing his guitar with a famous band. He was no doubt sleeping with every woman he encountered. Thankfully, I didn't care.

There were still plenty of tomatoes, but I lacked the will to pick and can them. I walked over to the raised bed, normally surrounded by brightly painted rocks. For some reason, they'd disappeared, exposing limp plants and bare ground. My first few months I so carefully steered clear of Frannie's prized berries. Now they showed the neglect of a beloved child who lost a parent. The Franniebells looked completely beyond redemption; Katherine would most likely have a magical concoction we could use to bring them back to life.

When I called Katherine out to look at them, she shook her head. "They've all lived a full life. You can dig up the whole bed and, in the fall, we'll mix in some manure, leaves, and sawdust. Gives everything a fresh start. We might even leave this space empty next spring to give the soil a rest."

"But these are Frannie's! Her test plots! We can't let them die!" My bottom lip trembled.

Katherine squeezed my shoulders. "Everything has a season, child. You can leave them 'til spring if you want, but I fear it will be easier to get rid of them now. Next year we'll put in a new bed somewhere else. These were Francine's special project."

You'll put your own stamp on this place."

"Your beautiful... rocks are... missing," I blubbered in between sobs, hoping she would give me the full story.

Katherine sighed. "I'm sure Francine is one step ahead of us, as usual. She knew how difficult it would be for us after she's gone, so she's removed them already."

I grasped the two plants firmly and yanked them from the ground. "Thank you for all you gave us, Franniebell." I took them and placed them in the compost pile without allowing myself to cry. It was the right thing to do; they gave Frannie the joy she deserved.

Through the screen door, I could hear Kyan, awake from his nap. Normally I would continue with what I was doing outside. But slowly I was learning to train myself for his cry.

I found my son, sitting up in the playpen in the living room. He flapped his arms excitedly when I walked in the door. "Is Mama's boy ready to get up?" I scooped him into my arms and kissed his now-slightly wavy hair.

Some days I looked at him and wondered who he resembled. He shared some of Kenneth's features, but when he grinned wide, his face resembled Edgar's. He was a beautiful boy, no matter what.

"Gigi? Can you bring the boy to me?" Frannie called weakly. Sometimes when he was less rambunctious, I would lay him on Frannie's chest in the recliner. I could tell she loved the feel of her grandson's body on hers and she said she was sure it was giving her a few extra hours of life.

Frannie's energy levels waxed and waned. Today she put on lipstick and combed her hair. She was propped up in the leather chair, the one she found the most comfortable in the house, with a pink, crocheted blanket tucked around her waist.

She raised her emaciated arms when she saw her grandson. "Is my punkin ready to see Grandma?" I set Kyan on her lap and kissed the top of her head. When I realized that Frannie could no longer hold the wiggling boy, I scooted the other chair close and put a hand on Kyan's back while Frannie snuggled him.

"I don't have many days left," Frannie announced, keeping her eyes on Kyan.

"Don't say that. We don't know. Look how good you're—"

"I know, hon. It doesn't do either of us any good to pretend otherwise."

We sat silently for a few minutes while Kyan grabbed at Frannie's hair.

"You've been so good to me. I had nowhere to go and no one to help me. I'll never be able to repay you. I just don't know how we'll survive without you. Though sometimes I worry about... things."

"Your old boyfriend, is what you mean?"

I gulped.

"That kind of person just takes and takes. He took your innocence and then he tried to take your dignity and your family."

Sometimes I thought she knew me better than I knew myself.

"Now you've built a good relationship with Ken. Those types—once they see that they can't squeeze any more from a person, they move on to a new, needy soul."

I thought about Lois and her night with Edgar. Something that would have kept me awake at night just a few months ago. Now it didn't seem that important.

"You're probably right. No doubt he's going wild in San Francisco."

Frannie smiled and nodded. "Don't spend another minute thinking about him. We've got more important things to discuss." She adjusted herself in the chair, trying to sit more upright.

"In each family, there is a keeper of secrets. It's not fair to burden everyone with them, so it takes a special family member to hold them all. Ever since I married Harlan, I've done that for the Brownwells."

I grabbed Kyan before he fell off Frannie's lap and set him on the floor. Normally, Frannie didn't allow him to crawl freely, but lately, he was becoming so restless sitting on laps that it seemed alright for just a few minutes.

"If you want to repay me, you can hold the secrets from now on. I'll tell you and they won't belong to me anymore."

I told Edgar everything Lois ever shared in confidence. Now I was a different person. A different woman. "What secrets?"

Frannie took a deep breath, which made her cough. I went to the kitchen to get some lemonade, but Katherine hadn't made any so I brought plain water. "Here."

"Never did I think having a coughing fit would take every bit of energy I had left for the day." Frannie took a sip and then sat back in her chair, closing her eyes for a minute. "Things have to be shared. It's part of your family history now."

I took her hand. "Whatever it is, I'm ready."

"I've told you about all of my struggles having a baby. And about beautiful little Eugenia." I nodded.

"Well, I changed the particulars of that story to suit the needs of my family. I held it in for all these years, hoping I would somehow forget. Losing a child is much worse than any cancer. The pain is so deep, you think you'll never heal, and maybe in the end that's a cancer that's festered in me all these years. Eugenia was my sweet, beautiful girl and I imagined her loss would kill me. I decided then and there she would be my last baby."

I furrowed my brow. "I don't understand. What about Kenneth?"

"Harlan's sister... Katherine found herself with a 'situation'. She fell in love with a man who married another woman. A taker, much like your Edgar. Katherine was devastated. When I found out she was pregnant... well, *you* know how women are treated when they are unmarried and with child. And she worked in the school system, where her condition would have meant her immediate dismissal."

My head was swirling. "What?"

"It was Harlan's idea. At first, I'm ashamed to admit, I wasn't about to have a woman in the 'family way' live in our home without the prospect of a husband. But then I thought, what do I care? I'm not beholden to anyone. She quit her job, told them she had family issues back in Pepperville, and moved in with us. I stayed home as well; I never left the farm for the rest of her pregnancy. Didn't want anyone getting strange ideas. We lived off what I'd canned that year and never went into town.

"Kenneth was born upstairs, right in your bed. Dr. Andrews came out and attended the birth. Didn't put Katherine's name on the birth certificate—her wishes. Katherine didn't even want to look at him. She handed him over to me and told me to make him the center of my world. That's just what I did. She went back to Moline and got her old job back the next year. Only the four of us knew."

"Kenneth's not your son? Does he know?" I tried picturing Kenneth growing up with Katherine, without Frannie's devotion.

Frannie snapped upright. "He *is* my son. He's my everything. There was never a reason to tell him differently." She laid her head back. "That's why I've been so careful over the years. Keeping the gossip in check. I never wanted my boy to be ashamed of where he came from."

Finally, I understood the strange dynamic in this home. Frannie's intense devotion to her son and invisible line of protection around this farm. Just as much to protect her as Kenneth.

"Now, you said you want to repay me. Well, first thing is that this family secret never gets out. It won't do anybody any good. And second," she grabbed my hand, "make Kyan the center of your world. There is nothing that comes before the boy. Not even his father. Focus your every thought on his well-being. You'll see what a fine man he'll become with that kind of attention. Just like my berries. Some love and attention and you've got the best in the county."

There was no use telling Frannie about her berries. "I will, I promise. And I'll take good care of Kenneth and Kyan. I won't let you down." I began to cry, as much as I was trying to be stoic.

"When you have more children, you'll have to figure

out how to divide your devotion. I never had to worry about that."

"I don't want any more children, Frannie. I can't do it without you. I would be a mess." The thought of doing this all over again made my heart race and my body sweat. Kyan was enough.

"You'll do just fine, hon. I've taught you well."

"No... I..." It hit me she wouldn't know whether she acquired more grandchildren or not.

"I'm sure you've had some thoughts about this second secret: the recipe for my strawberry jam. Lots of the normal things you'd find in a cookbook, but the crowning glory is black pepper and nutmeg. I never wrote it on the recipe card because I didn't want anyone to know. So many Snoopy Bettys come over to your kitchen and the first thing they do is search your recipes. A quarter teaspoon of each, just add 'til you can taste. That's a more closely guarded secret than the president's codes." Frannie smiled and nodded. "You'll be making it next summer."

Katherine will help." "Oh, Frannie." I sobbed.

"You'll plant your own berries one day. Give them a name that makes you happy. My garden gave me peace when all seemed lost. I think it did the same for you. Tell the university about my names though. They might want to use them in the future." She smiled weakly.

I wiped my tears and took her hand. "You've made me the woman I needed to be. Thank you."

We squeezed each other's hands. "Two secrets?" I couldn't believe this was the end of her confessions. So many years of police reports and investigations. "I can handle more. If you need to get them off your—"

She closed her eyes. "There are things that require a transfer of ownership. And then there are things that just need to remain where they are. I've made my peace. I need some rest. Call Katherine to come to help me to bed. Oh, and Gigi—if you need to plant some grass seed on what's left of the potato cellar, do it by yourself. No need to trouble Kenneth."

Chapter 26

Kenneth

TWO NIGHTS LATER, as my wife and I lay in a deep sleep in each other's embrace, there was a tap on the door. Kyan lifted his head but went back to sleep. I slid Gigi's arm off me carefully and opened the door. I didn't allow my father to speak. He collapsed in my arms.

"No, Dad. It can't be." I'd never seen Dad cry before. Georgina came over and wrapped her arms around us both.

Mom planned for her service to be held at the community center, but the Pepperville Pickle-It Society scheduled a major event there with vendors and every kind of pickled produce lined up on folding tables. Instead, we invited everyone to a potluck at Brownwell Farm. Dad found it too painful to hear words of remembrance, so he asked everyone to come with a happy memory of his wife to share.

I stood up and told the story of my first day of high school. "I didn't know anyone, and eventually my wife became my only friend." I smiled at Georgina, who was wearing the black dress and crocheted black sweater Mom bought her for just this occasion. She blew me a kiss.

"When I came home that afternoon, Mom takes one look at my face and says, 'All you need is one, son. One real friendship will get you through high school. Everything else becomes background noise.' She was right. I found my Gigi."

After the formal part, I flew Kyan, airplane-style, around the main rooms as Gigi helped Katherine slice boiled ham and smoked turkey in the kitchen. It felt more comfortable to stay busy than making small talk with people I barely knew. I could tell Gigi felt the same way. All these months later and Mom hadn't introduced Gigi to any of her friends.

I only paused for a minute to gaze at the newly framed picture hanging where the friendly cowboy used to be: the Franniebell plant, with its few, ripe, heart-shaped berries and the lush, green leaves it once possessed. Georgina took great photos she was so excited to share with Mom. I stayed up late for a few nights, staining wood for the perfect frame and then positioning the best picture just right behind it. I had it in my head Mom would hang on 'til she saw what we created. It was still sitting on a hidden bench in the big barn, waiting to be wrapped when Mom took her last breath.

When everyone was served, I sat down on the front porch for a few minutes with my wife, both of us hoping to clear our heads. Gigi leaned back, closing her eyes, and smiled. "Your mom picked out the best outfit.

I wish I could have seen that saleswoman's face when she came in and demanded a mint green pantsuit for burial."

"I told her once they should only serve mint chip ice cream to royal folks. She thought that was the funniest thing. Mom went right out and bought herself a top that looked like my ice cream. She saved that thing in the back of her closet for ten years."

"Georgina? You're looking well."

Chapter 27

Georgina

I OPENED MY eyes to see my mother standing in front of me, holding a casserole dish in her hands.

She was wearing her blue work shirt and pants. "Mom?" I rubbed my eyes to make sure it wasn't a dream. "What are you doing here?"

The year I spent babysitting my brothers, I wasn't interested in them. I ached for them now. To sit at our small kitchen table listening to mundane stories while the boys threw things at each other, like nothing had changed.

Mildred stared at the ground. "I decided I should pay my respects. This is a noodle and canned soup casserole." She handed the dish to me. "It's been quite some time, hasn't it?"

"I don't know what to say. It still doesn't make sense you're here. Did you have a relationship with Frannie?" I asked guardedly. I remembered her disparaging remarks about Frannie and other women of her income bracket.

"She came through my line every couple of weeks. Very frugal woman. Your father told me she brought you in to buy shoes. That was nice of her."

"My boy needs a diaper change." Kenneth stood up, hoisting Kyan on his shoulder. Mildred stared intently at Kyan for a moment and then returned her gaze to me.

Remembering Bob's disastrous meeting with Kyan, I didn't bother introducing my husband or my son. "Mom, I'm just... I don't know what you want."

Mildred pulled the other wooden rocker over close and climbed on it. "There have been some things that perhaps shouldn't have been said."

"I don't know... if I can forgive you."

Mildred chuckled. "I'm not here to ask for forgiveness. Good heavens, Georgina. You've had two husbands and you aren't even twenty."

I stood up. "I'll take your casserole inside. Thank you for coming."

"Wait." Mildred let out a loud sigh. "Let's try again. Maybe you didn't know, but Mrs. Brownwell offered me some money. When you moved out here with them, she said you didn't need to be upset by the likes of us. So, she said she'd pay us to stay away."

I sat back down. The thought of Frannie paying off my parents didn't shock me. She liked controlling everything in her world, including my parents.

"And did you take her money? To abandon your daughter?"

"We had to pay Mrs. Logan to take care of the boys after school. It was really a godsend. But you know, after taking her generous offer, we didn't have a choice. We couldn't come out and see you if we wanted." Mildred forced a smile.

"Which doesn't explain why you're here." I set the casserole dish down on the porch in front of her and resisted the urge to kick it. I doubted my family developed any plans to visit me, with or without Frannie's money.

"When I was in high school, I had a dear friend. She was my protector until she abruptly left."

"I know this story, Mom. She ran off, for whatever reason, and you were stuck trying to fend off bullies by yourself. I'm sorry that happened. But it had nothing to do with—"

"What you don't know is that she was also... in a family way."

My mouth dropped open. "You never knew what happened to her?"

"A young unmarried girl had no place in our home. My father made it clear she wasn't welcome and he was right. And I couldn't believe she had chosen this... situation... over our friendship. My sorrows all stemmed from her foolishness."

"Oh, Mom. This all makes sense now." I both hated and pitied my mother.

Mildred cleared her throat. "I have had some thoughts about seeing you now and then. I suppose some type of forgiveness would be in order. We are family."

I thought about all that I'd learned from Frannie and Katherine. How Frannie stressed putting Kyan before everything else. "I have to think about what's best for my son. Can I call you? Maybe at work, so Dad doesn't get upset?"

Kenneth came out to the porch with Kyan perched on one hip. "Clean and happy boy. He's about ready for his nap, though. I was thinkin' you might like to help me put him down." He put his hand on my shoulder and glanced at Mildred. "Is everything all right?"

"I just came to pay my respects. I'll be going now." She paused to stare at Kyan before standing. Her lips formed a perfunctory smile. "Georgina, you look strong and content."

When she made her way down the steps and through the mass of cars, Kenneth sat down next to me. "What was that about?"

"My mom... she thinks we're family now. Maybe not the kind of family that spends time together though."

"Hmm. What do you think about that?" He wrinkled his brow.

I looked into his eyes, Katherine's eyes. They were intensely concentrated on me. His lips were pulled tight with concern. No one else in my life cared so deeply for me. In his face I found home. He was love and stability, more than I had ever experienced. He would never leave my side. I was so lucky to have him, no matter how we got to this point. "You and Kyan. You are my family. And this farm. You're all I'll ever need."

BONUS Read

Those We've Forgotten

I pushed a strand of mocha-colored hair out of my mouth with one hand and swatted the flies away with the other. Summertime on the farm had its benefits and curses at the same time.

"Not so far, Kyan. Mommy needs to see you!" I called to my son, the light of my life.

Kyan Brownwell paused at the end of their gravel driveway. He pulled his feet off his pedals and twisted around, staring at his mother as if trying to decide if he would obey.

"Don't test me, son!"

I rubbed my growing belly, resentful once more that I had to go through another pregnancy. Though I was older this time, I wouldn't have the guidance and support of my mother-in-law, Francine.

"Another baby! We didn't think we could have any more. Kyan will make the best big brother!" Kenneth had been so excited to learn he would be a father again. He'd resigned himself to having one Brownwell to take over the farm, after years of trying for a sibling for Kyan. Though he'd grown up without brothers or sisters, he remembered how lonely he felt. Even with his mother's devotion, he needed someone else to share his life with.

"I'll start working on the nursery as soon as harvest is over!"

I hated that I couldn't share his enthusiasm.

Before Kyan's birth, my life had taken an unexpected turn for the worse. Now that I'd had Katherine and Frannie's guidance, I felt confident running the kitchen and the farm.

What I didn't feel especially excited about was another child. We were the perfect threesome the way they were. Kenneth and I attended Kyan's track meets and spelling bees, holding hands, proud that their boy was always the first in his class.

I'd invested all I had in this boy and had no desire to do it all over again.

I shaded my eyes when I heard a vehicle barreling down the gravel road. So close to supper, there were rarely any visitors.

When the large white pickup screeched to a halt, I pushed myself off the porch and walked over to it, hands on hips.

"Angela? What are you doing here so late in the day? I figured you'd be busy with the harvesters."

Angela Farriter and her husband, Bud, owned the farm closest to the massive Brownwell property, about a mile away. They always split the cost of the harvesters every summer. I was relieved to be done making meals for them and handing off that task to Angela.

Angela, also pregnant, but two months further along, rubbed her sundress-covered belly. "I had to talk to you about something. Can we go inside?"

Kyan rode his bike in front of me and glanced up at my face. "Hi, Mrs. Farriter."

"Hi, Kyan. I need to talk to your mom for a minute. Would it be okay if we go inside while you're riding?"

"Oh no, Angela. I never leave Kyan alone outside."

Angela shook her head. "Georgie, for Pete's sake. Your boy is almost ten years old. If he hasn't learned how to handle himself on a bicycle yet, it's time to call in reinforcements."

I gazed at my handsome son worriedly. "I don't know. It's just something my mother-in-law used to say. 'Always keep an eye on your boy. He's too precious to damage.' That stays with me."

"I'll be fine, Mom." Kyan reassured me. He pulled up on his handlebars and did a wheelie in the air.

"Kyan, I've told you over and over that's too dangerous!"

Angela took my arm and guided me up the stairs of the massive farm house.

I paused on the top step.

"Come on, Georgie. Five minutes. I'll time myself, I promise." Angela held the screen door open, watching two flies buzz inside.

We walked into the air conditioned mansion and I put my hands on my hips. "Time starts now."

"You know how we bought the property next to us?"

"Yes, two hundred acres from the Neville's. What about it?"

"Well, my Bud was out with the surveyor yesterday,

when the surveyor tripped and fell. After Bud helped him up, he realized it was an old tombstone."

"Oh?" My interest was piqued. "Do you know whose it was?"

"It's seen better days, I'm afraid. The only thing we could make out was the name 'Brownwell.' Do you know anything about that?"

I frowned. "The Brownwells have never owned that property, as far as I know. I can ask Kenneth when he comes in for supper."

"Please do. We don't want to start making improvements to the land until we know for sure who is buried there. Bad luck and all that."

There was a loud scream from outside and I shot Angela a quick, "told you so!" glance before rushing outside.

Kyan's bike was upside down and he was lying on the ground beside it.

"What happened to mommy's good boy? "I cooed. "Did you fall?"

Kyan cried, though no tears were coming from his eyes. "I was just riding in a circle and I fell."

Angela walked over to Kyan and pulled his bike to standing position. "Looks to me like you were doing wheelies, like your mom said not to."

Kyan put his tongue in his cheek and I glanced at him, shocked. "Kyan, is that what happened? You disobeyed me?"

Kyan kicked the rocks with his brand new tennis shoes but said nothing.

"You go inside, young man. Wash your hands for dinner. No more bike riding for tonight."

Kyan appeared as though he was going to argue with his mother, but thought better of it when he realized he had an observer.

When we both heard the bang of the door, I shaded my eyes. "How did you know that's what happened?"

"You should have known too. It's pure kid logic. Watch it, Georgie. If you let this kid get away with everything, he's going to be a terror as he gets older," I warned.

"Oh, that's nonsense. My mother-in-law said there's no such thing as spoiling a kid. She did the same with Kenneth and look how good he turned out?"

Angela rubbed her belly. "Kenneth is different. He worshipped the ground his mother walked on. I love Kyan like my own, but he reminds me of my third boy, Dennis. You never know what's happening behind your back."

"Tell me more about this grave." I motioned for Angela join me inside.

"I promised you it would only take five minutes and I'm holding myself to that." She opened her purse as we walked in and pulled out three pictures, handing them to me.

"I took these with the instant camera, so they are a little blurry. But you can clearly see the last name is Brownwell."

I squinted as I held a photo up to the light. "Looks like it says Fergus Brownwell. I don't think we have any relatives by that name."

We pivoted in unison when the kitchen door opened.

"'lo? Georgie? Are you upstairs?"

"In here, Kenneth! With Angela!"

Kenneth appeared in the doorway, a line of dirt rimming his forehead. He walked over to me and kissed me on the cheek.

"Pew, Kenneth! Did you bathe in oil today?" I playfully pushed him away.

"I felt like it. I knocked the oil pan over when I was changing the tractor oil. What's this picture?" He glanced over my shoulder.

"Fergus Brownwell? Never heard of him."

"That's just what I was telling Angela. It's in the corner of the new property they just bought."

"Do you think you could come over and take a look tomorrow, Kenneth? We want to till that soil, but my Brett is adamant we aren't disturbing that gravesite until we know more."

"Sure, I could do that. I'll stop before lunch." He turned to me with a look of concern. "Where's my boy?"

"He's upstairs, cleaning up. He had a little biking incident while we were visiting," I replied sheepishly.

"You left him out there all alone? What were you thinking?"

Kenneth darted upstairs and I shook my head. It bothered me to think Angela may be right. I thought of myself as a much better parent than she was.

"I'm going to have Brett talk to Ken. Your boy needs a little space or he'll resent you."

***

The old pickup rattled to a stop. It was the same truck Kenneth had used to pick me up on that fateful day that changed both of our lives. We had five newer vehicles and no real reason to keep this one, other than the sentimental value it held for them both.

Kenneth came around to the passenger side and opened the door, helping me to the ground.

"What an odd spot for a tombstone," I commented. Of all the rolling hills in Iowa, this one was particularly flat and unremarkable. "Knowing that your family came by the farm by happenstance, how would an earlier relative be buried right next door? Something isn't adding up."

Kenneth lifted his long legs high over the tall weeds, pausing when he realized I was struggling. He offered his hand and I took it with gratitude. After struggling across uneven ground, we maneuvered to the spot in the corner, where a small headstone rested.

I pulled a pencil and some notebook paper out of my pockets and knelt down so I could rub the pencil across the front. When I'd finished, I held it up to eye level. "Born 1831, Died 1848. He was just a kid, Kenneth! That makes this even more heartbreaking!"

"I wish Dad were here. He won't be on land until next Thursday."

"We shouldn't bother the man. It's the first big trip he's ever taken by himself. Kyan looks forward to his postcards from every port." I put my hands on my knees and rose. "I do have a thought, though. We still have your mother's family tree up in the attic. Would you mind getting it for me?"

"Sure. As long as you promise me something first."

I cocked my head to the side and studied my husband. "What would that be?"

"That whatever we find, we agree to bury Fergus in

the courtyard, with the rest of the family."

"Agreed. He was still a child. I was pregnant at that age and I know how immature my mind was."

Kenneth helped me through the weeds and back to the truck.

"What about his folks? Why would they leave him out here, all alone?"

***

The trunk containing all of Francine's carefully-documented family history occupied a corner space in a crowded attic. Her death was still too painful for us discuss with each other, let alone touch something she'd so lovingly crafted.

I sat a plate of warm brownies on the table and watched as Kyan put two in his mouth. "You won't be able to swallow all of that, son," I chided.

"I will too!" he retorted, spewing bits of brownies all over my freshly washed floor. When he'd finished, he opened his mouth and stuck his tongue out. "See? I told you."

"Go wash your hands, please. If you're going to handle Grandma's things, you'll need to be absolutely spotless."

Kyan took off on a dead run, almost knocking his father over. "Watch it, son!" Kenneth lifted the big book above Kyan's head and waited until he'd passed before setting it down on the table.

Unable to contain my enthusiasm, I opened the book and began rifling through.

"Careful, dear. You know mother put some delicate things in between some of the pages."

"Oh yes, I remember. Some of her embroidery, so

we'd remember–" I sucked in a breath and Kenneth put his arm around my and squeezed tightly.

"We'll find our Fergus and then the book will go back to its spot, where old hurts won't be brought up."

I nodded, carefully turning back to the first page.

"This picture of your great-great grandmother looks so much like your dad. She has the same big eyes and kind smile." I traced the picture of a woman wearing a high-collared black dress, wavy dark hair perched atop my head. "She was pretty."

"Annie Bing. I don't know that name either. Seems mom kept a few secrets."

I swallowed hard. "Your mom wouldn't keep anything from you if she hadn't felt it was important. Should we call your Aunt Katherine and ask what she knows?"

"By 'we' you me 'me', right? Gigi, you know how busy I am right now."

"No, Ken. I meant me. I've missed her since she moved back east."

"Mom! I'm hungry!"

"Okay, Kyan-Sweetie! Mommy will be down in a minute to get your supper!"

***

"I'm sure Francine would have told you if she wanted you to know," Katherine replied curtly.

While others might find her mannerisms abrupt, I still found them endearing, over a decade after our first meeting.

"They are going to dig up this grave, Katherine. I want to move him on to our property with the others and I'd like to have something to tell Kyan..." I paused,

245

rubbing the large lump on my abdomen, "the children," I corrected myself, "need to know their history."

Silence on the other end of the line didn't necessarily mean Katherine disapproved. I liked to take my time when replying. "All right. I'll tell you the story, and then we'll never speak of it again, yes, Georgina?"

"Of course."

"Well, Fergus and his parents rode the wagon out here from Pennsylvania. They were industrious, as were all the Brownwells. His father, Donald was a brickmaker who thought, what with all the new towns springing up, he could fill a void. On the long journey to Iowa, his wife and four children all contracted malaria and died. It was just he and Fergus who finally made their way to our fair state."

"Oh, that's sad! Poor Fergus!"

"Yes, well, I suppose."

I had grown used to Katherine's abrupt nature. Where others might be offended by it, I found it a comfort.

"There is no record of Fergus before his arrival, but one can assume he was incorrigible," Katherine continued. "To add to their misery, Donald soon realized he couldn't get his supplies because the rail line was still in its infancy. His orders came sporadically, when they didn't have more important freight to haul. Donald was forced to work at a livery stable to make ends meet. His son worked there as well, forgoing school.

Though he was a big help, Donald's son would often disappear for hours at a time, leaving Donald with the major share of work around their homestead. You see, Georgina, back then, folks had to have livestock and

246

grow all of their own food. It wasn't like things are today, where we can make a trip to the grocery store when something runs low."

"Yes, you're right, Katherine."

"When Donald asked Fergus why he'd run off, his reply was always vague. Donald had no time nor energy to curtail his wild teen, so instead he worked around him. Much like the teenagers of today, I'd wager."

"I'm assuming you know the real story? Where was Fergus all of this time?"

Katherine took a deep breath. Her dramatic pauses were more for herself than me, I imagined.

"He'd gotten himself wrapped up with the Duncan Gang."

"THE Duncan Gang? I learned about them in school!"

"The very same. They taught him how to steal cattle at night and that's just what he did. Over and over, until one evening a wise farmer waited in the grass. He and his hired hands stood and began shooting in the dark when they saw them coming. Fergus was shot in the arm."

"I bet his father was angry."

"More than angry. He kicked Fergus out. That's when Fergus began robbing trains with the Duncan Gang. By the time he returned to the Pepperville Territory, he'd made quite a name for himself as an outlaw."

"Why on earth would he return? He must've known he'd be caught."

"My suspicion is that he thought his father a simpleton. He could ride back into his life, bringing riches from his robberies and all would be forgiven. Well, things didn't turn out the way he'd planned. His father demanded Fergus leave, but instead, Fergus tied him up and threatened to shoot him. There were rumors the boy was visiting his father, as someone in town had recognized him at the bar the night before. They all came out and surrounded the house. Shooting everything they had."

"And that's how Fergus died?"

"That's how Donald died. Fergus refused to give up, so they charged the house and drug him out. He was strung up on a tree and buried in the pasture."

I thought for a moment. "But how were there more Brownwells if everyone died? And how is it that there is an actual grave marker? You would think they wouldn't want any trace of Fergus."

"To answer both of your questions, young Fergus had been sowing his oats. There was a young woman who had two children by him. The lad was only seventeen, so I shudder to think how that worked."

I shuddered too. Katherine often forgot I was that age when I had Kyan.

"The reason there was a tombstone, was that no crops were to be planted in that area, lest they be cursed with a bad yield. They were very superstitious back then."

It was going to be difficult to pursuade Kenneth to bury a criminal of this magnitude in the family cemetery, beside his beloved mother and grandmother.

"Is there anything else? For some reason, I want to know more about Fergus. Maybe because I was motherless at his age. I know how you can fall off the rails."

"Georgina, you were nothing like this scoundrel.

Your heart was always in the right place. I don't think young Fergus had a decent bone in his body."

After assuring Katherine there would be no more upsetting talk of family black sheep, I hung up and returned to the attic in search of more information.

I dug through piles and piles of Kenneth's clothing and report cards; there wasn't one unremarkable event in his childhood Frannie had missed. For a moment, I felt guilty I hadn't documented my own son's life in such detail.

When I finished, I searched the attic on my knees, trying to discover where else Frannie may have hidden family history.

It struck me that the portrait hanging over the living room fireplace had always seemed out of place. I hoped Kenneth wouldn't come in from the fields for lunch early. He would have too many questions I didn't want to answer.

Dragging Frannie's multi-purpose stool from the kitchen across the threshold and into the living room, I climbed it carefully. Pregnancy left me off-balance, one of its many detriments.

Carefully, I lifted the painting and very nearly fell off the stool trying to lower it to the ground. I was on the last step, relieved I'd made it, when the phone rang, startling me. I leaned backward and the painting fell to the ground with me on top of it.

The beautiful pine frame splintered and the picture tore in two places. Inside, I was pleased I could hang something in its place. It had been an eyesore to me ever since a new home décor store opened and I was exposed to vibrant, colorful art.

I turned the painting over. Taped to the back were several, yellowed documents. I unsecured them, opening the pages with the same care I used when cleaning Frannie's best China.

They were three pages, written by someone with exquisite handwriting; long loopy cursive in straight lines.

December 2nd, 1885

School Marm Miss Johnson says we are to compose an essay about a person we should admire. I decided I would write three. When I'm finished, I'll submit one and keep the others for my own hope chest. The first one, about my mother. She raised my brother Seamus and myself quite properly, after being widowed at the age of eighteen.

Mother cleaned homes, took in mending, sold eggs, whatever it took to keep us suitably fed and clothed.

She only married again for love at age thirty-five. Her hands were curled by years of sewing and her eyesight poor. She was surprised anyone would give her a second look, but Mother was a beauty, no matter how hard she lived. Mr. James Farritor came to town in need of a governess for his two young boys. They were wild and untamed, but Mother found them irresistible, after my own nature.

We moved in with Mr. Farritor and he took a liking to my brother and myself. He told me first that he was sweet on Mother. Me, being protective, I needed to make sure his intentions were proper before agreeing to them.

He and Mother were married in the courtyard of his home two months later. Three more children followed, but Mother never lost her cheerful spirit nor her willingness to help us children with our school work. She stayed up well past everyone else, darning clothing making us the finest lunches and pressing the girls' pinafores.

Mother died just last fall. Mr. Farritor, whom I now refer to as father, said we must bury mother next to her first husband, as that's what is proper. It was at this time I asked the true nature of my father's life and death. Mother was reluctant to tell me and I never wanted to make me cross.

What I learned changed my opinion of both my mother and my father.

Sincerely,

Abigail Brownwell

I set the paper down, stunned by what I'd read. There had to be a reason Frannie hid these papers. Didn't I want my husband to know he'd had such courageous women in his lineage?

Though I was eager to read the other two, I knew Kyan would be expecting his afternoon snack when he got off the bus from school. I'd just recently begun allowing him to ride the bus, after much persuading from both he and his best friend, Angela's son.

I liked to give him something hearty after he'd been working so hard all day, so I often prepared a full meal. He didn't like cafeteria food and this way I knew he'd eat something substantial.

When I'd finished making an egg salad sandwich, sliced fruit and freshly baked cookies, I lowered myself down to the floor again to read the next letter:

December 3rd, 1885

My grandfather, Donald Brownwell was a brave man. He traveled all the way from Pennsylvania to Iowa with little more than the clothes on his back. On the way, his wife and all but one of his children died of malaria.

Heartbroken, grandfather found the courage to carry on and build a business on his own. A mason of excellent quality, he had trouble finding materials to make his bricks on the desolate Iowa plains.

That's when he came up with a plan: he would get a job operating the barge himself, adding his own supplies to the load. For six months, he worked the barges, happy to have found a way to build the business he'd dreamt of.

One day, his boss paid a surprise visit to the dock and saw the extra cargo. Grandfather was fired on the spot, not even allowed to take what he'd paid for and rightly owned along with him.

Fergus, meanwhile worked in the fields of their closest neighbor, contributing everything he could to the family business. One night as he road home with only the moonlight to guide him, he was accosted by the evil Duncan Gang. They roamed the countryside, terrorizing rural dwellers by stealing their livestock and burning their homes to the ground. Fergus, as luck would have it, had just been paid.

He begged the Duncan Gang to leave him with a few pennies to contribute to his father's business, knowing they had nothing to eat and nothing to live on.

They agreed to return one dollar. If he wanted more, he'd have to work for them. Fergus had no choice.

He terrorized women and children, stole horses and robbed trains. All for the money he was owed. One day, the Duncan Gang handed Fergus the cash he was waiting on and more. They said his debt had been paid and he was free to go.

His trusting nature was what got him killed.

The law had recently discovered it was the Duncan Gang behind all of the recent crimes. They decided to ride north, but first, left all of the evidence in the hands of Fergus Brownwell, along with a note given to the sheriff by a young boy who was paid with a shiny new penny. The note was a "confession" by Fergus.

He couldn't take the strain of his life anymore and wanted to give up, but would only do so if they came to his door.

That was the day every law man in two counties road out to the humble Brownwell abode, guns blazing.

At first, Grandfather thought they had come to collect all the salary he'd been paid on the barge. He instructed Fergus to ignore the calls for his surrender, as he'd seen this tactic used before to get the real perpetrator agree to give up.

When the law men began reading off the charges against Fergus, Grandfather was shocked and upset. Fergus tried explaining to his father, but it was to no avail. Grandfather took Fergus's hat, placed it on his own head, and stood.

Fergus yelled, "no, Pa!"

It was too late. Grandfather was felled by a hail of bullets.

The law men said they were coming in, thinking Grandfather was Fergus and he was now deceased. In a panic, Fergus met them at the door, where they tied him and drug him away to his death.

You may ask how I know all of this information, given the players involved are deceased?

Grandfather and Fergus weren't the only ones present in the home at the time. My mother, myself and my brother were hiding in the cellar just below the kitchen.

Sincerely,

Abigail Brownwell

I decided to wait until the following morning to read the last letter. I needed to talk to Kenneth, though I wasn't sure what, exactly, I would say. He had plenty of noteworthy people in his family, that part wouldn't surprise him. No one though, who had sacrificed their life for their child.

The three of us devoured our barbecued chicken and corn-on-the-cob with our usual conversation.

"Did you have a good day, son?" Kenneth asked.

"Yeah. I'm going to the county spelling bee. Me and Lucy Bennet. She's the alternate." Kyan rolled his eyes at his father, his milk mustache framing his adorable mouth.

"You'll be nice to her, son. We treat women with the respect they deserve." Kenneth glanced at me and winked, squeezing my knee underneath the table.

"Ken, I was doing some redecorating today. You know, that painting in the casual living room has always bothered me."

His eyes widened. "Mom picked that out!"

"I know. I don't want to get rid of it. I'd just like to

rotate it in and out. Maybe hang something a little more colorful in its place for a while. Would that be okay with you?"

"Doesn't bother me any."

That was what he said when he really was bothered. It was too late to undo the damage I'd done, so he'd just have to live with this change.

"Today, I took it down, just to see what I'd like to fill the space."

"Georgie, you shouldn't be up on a ladder in your condition! Why didn't you just wait for me to get home and do it for you?"

"Mom, when we did the health and safety check last month, we agreed you wouldn't be up on ladders!"

"Kyan, let me get this out!" Sometimes as the only female, I didn't feel heard.

"I found three letters from your relative Abigail. The story she tells is remarkable."

"Oh?" he replied, more interested in his food than in what I was saying.

"I'd like to read them to you, if you wouldn't mind."

Kyan fidgeted in his seat. "May I be excused?"

I was slightly hurt he wasn't interested, but it wasn't the end of the world. We'd explain it all to him when he was older.

"Yes, get your homework done and I'll be up to help with your bath."

When he'd left the room, Kenneth gave me the look.

"I know. He's too old for his mother to help with his baths. It's so hard to let him grow up, Kenneth."

He rubbed my shoulder. "You've been a wonderful

mother to him. And you'll be just as good with this next one."

I swallowed hard. I wasn't sure I had anything left in me to give another child. I never wanted Kenneth to know though.

I read through one letter and then the second.

When I finished, I looked up at Kenneth. "Can you believe it?" Part of me worried he might be angry that I'd unearthed something Frannie meant to remain hidden.

"Don't keep me in suspense, read the last one!" he replied, much to my relief.

"I haven't even read it myself yet."

"Let's go sit where you can be more comfortable."

I didn't want him to see the mess I'd created of Francine's picture, so I suggested the porch we'd recently enclosed to keep the mosquitoes out. It had a lovely swinging bench.

Once we were settled and my aching feet were propped on Kenneth's lap, I began reading:

December 4th, 1885

Fergus was a hero, that was true. But I fear he was much too young to become a father. Mother says it was love at first sight when he saw her in the general store. Lavinia Stockton had waist-length thick brown hair and grey eyes that changed color with the seasons. Her father expected her to marry someone of prominence in the community, so that first day, when she was sweeping behind the counter, her eyes were trained on something other than Fergus.

There was no denying the electricity between them. They'd steal moments behind the store, in the barn, wherever providence would allow. Fergus promised that once the brick business was well established, he would go to her father and ask for her hand in marriage.

With that in mind, when Lavinia discovered she was with child, she assumed Fergus would have the means to show her father he was suited for her hand. Instead, Fergus lost his money to the Duncan Gang and the brick business never took off.

Mother was sent to live with relatives in Nebraska in disgrace. She never admitted to her parents my parentage, but they must've had some idea.

On his many travels across the Iowa Territory and beyond, Fergus stopped to see Mother and his new daughter. On one such trip, they escaped in the night and exchanged vows.

By then, Mother was expecting[1] my brother. On their wedding night, Father confessed his deeds. He felt such shame, but didn't see a way out. He was certain the day would come when he could take his wife and children to live a respectable life in Iowa.

When I was four years old, Mother could take the separation no longer. We got on a train and rode to Pepperville Territory, where Father greeted us at the station. Mother was still afraid of her parents, so we had to be careful we weren't seen. Father prepared a lovely space for us in the cool cellar underneath the house. It wasn't bad, we had plenty of room to move around, and at night, he would come down and play songs on his guitar.

At first, Grandfather had no idea we were there. But one night, my brother Seamus wandered upstairs as Grandfather was sleeping in his chair by the fire. He hopped right up on Grandfather's lap and made himself comfortable. That's how our wonderful memories with grandfather began.

He understood why we all needed to stay hidden. Between the dangerous Duncan Gang and Mother's angry parents, we didn't know from one day to the next what might happen to us. So we stayed under the house by day and our family sat together by the fire at night.

That day, the day I lost half my world, We were darning socks when we heard a terrible noise. Mother knew better than to let us go upstairs. Instead, we waited quietly in the cellar. I put my ear up to the trap door and heard as grandfather uttered his last words.

Then I heard a flurry of shots.

Mother pulled me away and put her hand over my mouth. Her other hand was previously occupied with Seamus's mouth. When it had been quiet for some time, we cautiously opened the door.

I saw Grandfather in the corner, bloodied with a vacant stare. Mother ordered me to throw a blanket over him. She got the cash Father hid in the cellar, cash the Duncan Gang didn't know he'd kept. We left on the next train.

You see, I've been surrounded by brave souls my entire existence.

Sincerely,

Abigail Brownwell

Kenneth shook his head.

"All I know is, we've got to take Fergus and bury him on our property. And it sounds like his wife is buried there too."

"I bet her name isn't on the tombstone because she

didn't want her children to experience any fallout from the Brownwell name."

"Tomorrow I'm going to call the excavating company. We'll take both of those bodies and bury them next to the rest of the family, where they belong."

It was hot and muggy fall day when we put the long lost members of our family in their rightful resting place. Kenneth hired a four-piece orchestra and a catering company supplied an assortment of sand-wiches, fruits and cakes. It was the most elaborate funeral I'd ever attended, even moreso than Frannie's.

It was well attended by those in our community, most out of pure curiosity. It didn't matter to us, as long as they were there to give Fergus a fitting send off.

Katherine refused to attend. "That's stuff and nonsense," she said curtly when we'd called. "Tales of the Old West, nothing more. I've never heard of any of these people."

Kenneth gave the eulogy, telling our friends and neighbors in attendance the story of Fergus Brownwell. There wasn't a dry eye in the house when he'd finished. He held his hand out, motioning for Kyan and I to join him in front of the crowd.

"The reason we gathered today was to celebrate family," he concluded. "The Brownwells are lucky to have such a rich history and a bright future. This isn't the last you'll be hearing from us."

About the Author

USA TODAY Bestselling Author, Joann Keder spent her first forty-five formative years on the Great Plains of Nebraska. A midlife move to the Pacific Northwest lead her to re-examine her priorities. She began releasing all of the stories that had been percolating inside her head and now it appears there's no stopping the flood. Writing, hiking and eating chocolate are her passions. Not necessarily in that order.

www.ingramcontent.com/pod-product-compliance
Lightning Source LLC
Chambersburg PA
CBHW021615120626
46545CB00001B/241